Bible Studies on the Overcoming Life

by Bob and Rose Weiner

*"For I am not ashamed of the gospel,
...for in it the righteousness of God is revealed from faith to faith..."*

Romans 1:16-17

MARANATHA PUBLICATIONS

P.O. Box 1799
Gainseville, FL 32602

website: http://www.mpi2000.net

Cover Photograph by Jerry Sieve

Unless otherwise noted, all Scripture quotations are from the New American Standard Version of the Bible. Copyright © The Lockman Foundation 1960, 1962, 1963, 1968, 1971, 1973, 1975, 1977. Used by permission.

Printed in the United States of America
International Standard Book Number: 0-938558-01-3

Preface

Bible Studies on the Overcoming Life has been prepared to enable you to discover precious truths from God's Word which will help you to be a victorious overcomer. For some of the material we were greatly inspired by some of the ideas in the classic book *Release of the Spirit* by Watchman Nee. We wish to credit Mr. Nee for the valuable impartation he left us. Mr. Nee's material is used with permission from the publisher.

To these thoughts we have added more studies from God's Word on the related subjects of righteousness and practical Christian living, tying in the role and importance of faith to these themes.

The book is concluded with several studies on ministering to others in the power of the Spirit, building on the foundations laid in the previous chapters.

As you study God's Word, we pray that you will grow in grace and experience the overcoming life!

Bible Studies
On the Overcoming Life

Table of Contents

SERIES I

BROKENNESS

"That I may know Him, and the power of His resurrection
and the fellowship of His sufferings,
being made conformed to His death."

Philippians 3:10

"Unless a grain of wheat falls into the earth and dies,
It remains by itself alone;
but if it dies, it bears much fruit."

John 12:24

SERIES I
BROKENNESS
STUDY 1—THE PATH OF THE CROSS

The basic lesson every servant of God must learn is that any measure of fruitfulness requires the breaking of the carnal (fleshly) part of us (I Cor. 3:2-3). This allows *the release of our spirit*.

"Often we hear about the cross. Perhaps we are too familiar with the term. But what is the cross after all? When we really understand the cross, we shall see it means the breaking of the outward (carnal) man."[1] The cross reduces the carnal man to death and splits open the human shell. "The cross must break all that belongs to the (carnal) man-our opinions, our ways, our cleverness, our self love,..."[2] anything that is not controlled by the Spirit.

As we allow the cross to work in our lives, we become transparent. There is no one more beautiful than one who is broken! Stubborness and self-love give way to beauty in those who have been broken by God. "Once the carnal man is broken, man's spirit very naturally abides in the presence of God..."[3] "Without effort our spirit can receive divine revelation. When we are witnessing or preaching, we send forth God's Word through our spirit. Furthermore, we may spontaneously contact the spirit in others by our spirit. Whenever one speaks in our pressence, we can... evaluate what kind of person he is, what attitude he is taking,... and what his need is... With the breaking of the... (carnal) man, the spirit begins to flow and is ever open the others."[4]

This is not an easy path. This is a death of self, so that the Spirit of God that dwells in our spirit might come forth. Then the fullness of God can be given through our lives to a lost and dying world. This is the only path to being wholly led by the Spirit. This is the path Christ calls His disciples to follow. This is the way of the overcomers.

1. What requirement does Jesus lay down for those who want to be His disciples? (Luke 14:27)

   _____

2. What was another way that Jesus and Paul described this requirement? (Matt. 10:39; Phil. 1:21)
   a _____
   b _____

3. What does Paul say is our reasonable service as Christians? (Rom. 12:1-2)
   a _____
   b _____
   c _____

4. We are commanded to have the "mind" in us which was also in Christ Jesus. What is this "mind" according to Philippians 2:5-9?
   a _____
   b _____
   c _____
   d _____

5. Why are we able to experience the likeness of Christ's resurrection in our life? (Rom. 6:5)

   _____

6. Who is the one that is able to produce fruit, according to John 12:24?

   _____

7. If we submit ourselves to this cross, what are we promised? (II Tim. 2:11-12)
   a _____
   b _____

[1]Release of the Spirit, Watchman Nee, Sure Foundation, Cloverdale, Ind. p. 14, Used by permission.
[2]Ibid, p. 14
[3]Ibid, p. 23
[4]Ibid, p. 23

8. What does Jesus call this death experience? (Matt. 3:11)

_____

9. How will the Lord appear to those who submit to this death? (Note: Though addressed to Israel, the spiritual application is pertinent for Christian believers.) (Mal. 3:1-3)

a _____

b _____

c _____

10. What will He do to these saints? (Mal. 3:3)

a _____

b _____

11. What is the purpose of this refining fire? (Mal. 3:3)

_____

12. The mother of two of the disciples requested that her sons might sit with Christ upon His throne. What question did Christ ask them? (Matt. 20:20-23; Mark 10:35-40)

a _____

b _____

13. This is what Christ is asking us today. We all want to reign with Him upon His throne—but are we willing to drink of His cup, and to undergo the baptism that Christ went through—even *death to self* upon the cross? Jesus Himself wrestled with this question in the Garden of Gethsemane. What decision did He make? (Matt. 26:39,42; John 18:11)

_____

14. We too must decide whether we will "drink the cup." This is the path of suffering, sprinkled with blood, but also one of joy. What was Jesus' attitude toward the cross? (Heb. 12:2)

_____

15. We see also the great champions of faith in the Old Testament had this same attitude. What is said of Moses in Heb. 11:24-26?

a _____

b _____

c _____

The crucified life involves these aspects of suffering which break us and purge us: the endurance of personal trials, suffering on behalf of others, and sharing in Christ's sufferings.

—NOTES—

SERIES I
BROKENNESS
STUDY 2—THE ENDURANCE OF PERSONAL TRIALS

1. What does James say is the purpose of trials? (James 1:2-4)

   a _____

   b _____

   c _____

2. What does James say your attitude should be toward trials? (James 1:2-4)

   a _____

   b _____

3. What will those who endure these trials receive? (James 1:12)

   _____

4. How does Peter describe these trials? (I Peter 1:6-7)

   a _____

   b _____

   c _____

5. What does he tell you to do? (I Peter 1:6)

   _____

6. What is the trial of your faith worth to you? (I Peter 1:7)

   _____

7. What is the reason for this trial of fire? (I Peter 1:7; II Thess. 1:4-5)

   a _____

   b _____

8. The apostles also went through these trials. How does Paul describe these testings? (II Cor. 1:8-9)

   _____

   _____

9. What did Paul say was the purpose of these trials? (II Cor. 1:9)

   _____

10. What treasure do we have in earthen vessels? (II Cor. 4:6-7)

    _____

11. Paul says that we have this treasure in *earthen vessels*, in order that God's great power may be evident (II Cor. 4:7). The "earthiness" of our vessels is apparent in our being "broken." How does Paul describe this means of being broken? (II Cor. 4:8-9)

    a _____

    b _____

    c _____

    d _____

12. What does Paul call this experience? (II Cor. 4:10)

_____

13. What was the purpose of being delivered unto this death? (II Cor. 4:10-11)

_____

—NOTES—

SERIES I
BROKENNESS
STUDY 3—SUFFERING ON BEHALF OF OTHERS

1. The second phase of crucifixion is suffering on behalf of others. What are the strong called to do, and what should their attitude be? (Rom. 15:1)

   a _____

   b _____

2. How are we supposed to help our brethren that are going through trials? (II Cor. 1:3-5)

   _____

   _____

3. What are the strong to do with their weaker brothers? (Gal. 6:1-2)

   a _____

   b _____

4. Jeremiah, a prophet of God, suffered greatly for the sins of his people. What was his experience? (Lam. 3:48-49)

   _____

   _____

5. Jesus too lamented greatly over His people. What was His experience? (Matt. 23:37; Luke 19:41)

   _____

   _____

6. How did the apostle Paul suffer because of his concern for unbelieving Jews? (Rom. 9:1-3)

   _____

7. How did Paul serve the Lord when facing opposition in bringing the gospel to those living in the province of Asia? (Acts 20:18-21)

   _____

If you continue in the pathway of the cross, you too will know this suffering and brokenness of heart for people that reject the truth and you too will mourn over their sin.

—NOTES—

SERIES I
BROKENNESS
STUDY 4—SHARING IN THE SUFFERING OF CHRIST

1. The third phase of crucifixion and the highest form of suffering is to suffer on behalf of Christ. The reproaches which fell upon Christ will fall upon you. What are we called to do according to Philippians 1:29?

_____

2. How can we expect the world to respond to us if we partake of His sufferings? (John 15:18-21; Luke 6:22-23)
   a _____
   b _____
   c _____
   d _____
   e _____

3. This is experiencing the fellowship of His sufferings. If we experience this what will happen? (Phil. 3:10-11)

_____

4. What does Peter exhort us to do when this happens? (I Peter 4:12-13)

_____

5. Why should we rejoice? (I Peter 4:14)

_____

Is this not the character of brokenness, to have the Spirit of Christ flowing through you so fully that the world actually attacks, not you, but the Spirit of Christ in you?

6. Christ was our example. Did He go through trials? (Heb. 4:15)

_____

7. How did Christ learn obedience? (Heb. 5:8-9)

_____

8. a How was Christ made perfect? (Heb. 2:10)

_____

   b Can we expect to come into perfection (maturity) without this?

_____

Read I Peter 2:18-23.

9. Why did Christ leave us this example? (I Peter 2:21)

_____

10. What wins God's approval? (I Peter 2:19-20)
   a _____
   b _____

11. What did Jesus do when going through these persecutions? (I Peter 2:23)

a _____

b _____

c _____

d Did He try to get out of His trials or defend Himself?

_____

12. Paul also knew this. He did not try to escape the trials, but received them gladly from the hand of the Father. Why? (Rom. 8:17-18)

a _____

b _____

13. What does Paul call the revelation of this glory in us? (Rom. 8:19) This will happen when we are resurrected at Christ's return (Rom. 8:21-23).

_____

In order to become sons, we must experience what is written in Hebrews 12:2-13. Read this passage.

14. If you become faint and begin to become discouraged through trials, what should you remember? (Heb. 12:3-7)

a _____

b _____

c _____

d _____

15. If we do not experience such trials or discipline from the Lord, then what are we? (Heb. 12:8)

_____

16. Why does God discipline and correct us? (Heb. 12:10)

_____

17. If we yield to God's discipline, what will be the result? (Heb. 12:11)

_____

18. When we suffer persecution, what makes us worthy of the kingdom of God? (II Thess. 1:4-5)

_____

19. Then what saying will come true? (Rev. 12:10)

a _____

b _____

c _____

d _____

20. These are they that overcome. How did they overcome? (Rev. 12:11)

a _____

b _____

c _____

21. What promise do we have if we overcome? (Rev. 3:21)

_____

Let us then choose rather to suffer affliction with the people of God, esteeming the reproach of Christ better than riches, and for the joy that is set before us, let us endure the cross, and sit down with Christ on the throne of God.

MEMORY VERSE: Philippians 3:10-11

_____
_____
_____
_____

—NOTES—

STUDY 5—GOD'S PURPOSE IN TRIALS AND THE SPIRITUAL PROMISED LAND

1. Why did God bring Israel out of the house of bondage in Egypt? (Deut. 6:22-23) According to Hebrews 3-4, the Israelites' entrance into Canaan is a type of our entering God's rest. Therefore, God brought *us* out of "Egypt" (the world) in order that we might receive our "promised land" of rest in God.

   _____

2. What is the difference between the unredeemed person's ways and God's ways? (Isa. 55:8-9)

   _____

3. Therefore, what does God promise to do for His people? (Isa. 48:17)
   a _____
   b _____

4. God lays before His people two paths. What are these in the language of Isaiah 1:19-20?
   a _____
   b _____

We see these promises fulfilled in Israel's journey through the wilderness. They had the promises of God, but because of unbelief they perished in the wilderness. Only two men, Joshua and Caleb, who dared to believe that God would give them the land, who were willing and obedient, entered in from that generation.

5. Now we know that the things that happened to Israel happened for our example. We see that Israel in the natural is a picture of spiritual Israel. What does the Scripture say concerning this? (I Cor. 10:11)

   _____

   _____

We see in natural Israel a picture of those things which are for us.
   1. Israel was delivered from the bondage of Egypt, receiving the promise of a land flowing with milk and honey.
   2. They crossed the Red Sea, being miraculously delivered from Pharaoh's army.
   3. They wandered in the wilderness for forty years. (This is longer than God had planned, they wandered because of unbelief. It only took Jesus forty days to do in the wilderness what it took Israel to do in forty years.)
   4. They entered into the promised land and took it little by little—God driving out their enemies from before them one by one.
   This is the pattern of natural Israel. We see the pattern repeated in spiritual Israel in Romans.
   1. Romans 5—Deliverance from bondage of the world and receiving the promises.
   2. Romans 6—Water baptism (deliverance and burial of the old creation).
   3. Romans 7—The wilderness.
   4. Romans 8—The promised land.
   Let us look briefly at these chapters.

Romans 5—The Promise

6. Having been justified by faith, what do we stand doing? (Rom. 5:2)

   _____

   _____

7. As Israel left Egypt, in what "hope" were they rejoicing? (Deut. 8:7-9)

_____

_____

8. What other promise do we have? (Rom. 5:17)

_____

Romans 6—Burial of the Old Creation

9. As the children of Israel were led through the Red Sea and the ones who held them in bondage were buried in the water, what provision do we have for the old creation which has held us in bondage to sin? (Rom. 6:4; Col. 2:12)

_____

_____

10. What is our condition as we enter into the wilderness, holding fast to the promises of God? (Rom. 6:22)

a _____

b _____

c _____

d _____

Romans 7—The Wilderness

11. Now having received the promises of God, we enter into the wilderness experience which could also be called the trials and testings of God. For example, if we have the promise that "God will supply all of our needs according to His riches in glory by Christ Jesus"—after we have received this promise we enter into the wilderness of testing. As we observe the reasons for Israel's wilderness testing, what purposes may be seen for our trials? (Deut. 8:1-6)

a _____

b _____

c _____

d _____

e _____

f _____

g _____

12. How is this wilderness described? (Deut. 8:15)

a _____

b _____

c _____

d _____

e _____

f _____

g _____

13. God sent spies into the promised land. Ten men came back with an evil report and two men came back with a good report. What was the good report? (Num. 13:30)

a _____

b _____

What was the evil report? (Num. 13:31-33)

a _____

b _____

c _____

14. As a result of this, what did Israel do? (Num. 14:1-4)

_____

15. Caleb and Joshua were willing and obedient and even in the midst of the trial they believed God's Word. The others refused and rebelled in unbelief. As a result what happened? (Num. 14:22-24)

a _____

b _____

16. In Romans 7, we see a man going through the spiritual wilderness of God's testings. What is the problem here? (Rom. 7:15)

_____

17. After all this battle and struggle, to what conclusion does he come? (Rom. 7:24-25; 8:1-2)

_____

18. What two exhortations do we have to encourage us while our faith in God's promises are being tried?

a (I Tim. 6:12) _____

b (Heb. 10:23) _____

Romans 8—The Promised Land

19. Now we come to Romans 8 which is the spiritual promised land, a land in which we can reign as kings in life. What are 21 promises of this land?

1. (v. 1) _____

2. (v. 2) _____

3. (v. 4) _____

4. (v. 6) _____

5. (v. 9) _____

6. (v. 11) _____

7. (v. 13) _____

8. (v. 14) _____

9. (v. 15) _____

10. (v. 16) _____

11. (v. 17) _____

12. (v. 21) _____

13. (v. 23) _____

14. (v. 26) _____

15. (v. 28) _____

16. (v. 29) _____

17. (v. 31) _____

18. (v. 32) _____

19. (v. 34) _____

20. (v. 35) _____

21. (v. 37) _____

20. How did Israel take the promised land? (Ex. 23:29-30)

_____

21. After considering Israel's experience, why might it be that we do not experience all the blessings which God has for us at once? (Deut. 8:10-14)

a _____

b _____

There are many examples in Scripture of those who received God's promises and were tried. Some stood fast and entered into the promises and others failed. Here are two such examples:

Adam and Eve received *the promise,* "You can have the whole Garden, except don't eat of the tree of the knowledge of good and evil." Their *wilderness* of testing, Satan tested them. *Result,* they lost the promise—they did not stand in the face of trial.

Job, the elders of the gates bowed down to him. His *wilderness* of testing, all was stripped from him, yet he stood fast in the promises of God. *Result,* God increased his later end greater than his beginning.

Here is one final example. Israel left Egypt with the promises of God in front of them and Pharaoh coming up behind them. Pharaoh was drowned with his army in the Red Sea and the whole company of Israel, safe on the other side, danced before the Lord and sang the song of victory. Three days later, after God's mighty provision, they ran into some bitter water and murmured against God. Applying Israel's experience, we can take three alternatives to crossing our *wilderness.*

First alternative: extend your visit in the wilderness, failing the same thing over and over again.

Second alternative: to perish, your bones bleaching in the wilderness.

Third alternative: to stand and enter—standing with the promise through the problem—and enter into God's provision.

22. Jesus went right across the wilderness. He stood in the face of adversity and held fast to the Word of God. It is written of Him in Isaiah that His portion is to be with the great. With whom will Jesus divide the spoil? (Isa. 53:12)

_____

_____

—NOTES—

The Holy Spirit is moving upon the whole Body of Christ, the Church, and is raising up a people to meet the challenge of this day—a people who will *live* and *walk* in what God *says* they are spiritually. For God has called us not to live in what we were, but in what He has made us. God wants you to *live* in the reality, the blessing, the fulness, and the power of communion with the Ascended Lord. This is a *faith* position. If you will grasp it, and take it, the Holy Ghost will teach you how to abide or rest in your position until it becomes a fact and a reality in your everyday experience.

The spiritual man is freed from trying to receive what he already possesses according to God's Word. Many have spent all their time trying to suppress the "old man" and keeping him under foot. They have spent all their time confessing and hanging around the cross—when they should be reckoning the "old man" dead, and rejoicing as they are seated together in heavenly places with Jesus. We are only going to get through the dark hours that will close this age as we live in the light of the glory of the fellowship with the Ascended Lord. The spiritual man's aim is to this end, to bring revelation and manifestation of Christ. When Christ returns, He will be coming for His Church that is living and walking in the Spirit, in all that God says it is, has, and can do. It will be noticed by the world and by the Lord that the Church is without "spot or blemish."

1. What does the Bible say about the "new life" of us who have been born again by the Spirit? (II Cor. 5:17)

   _____

2. What has happened to our "old life"? (II Cor. 5:17)

   _____

3. What has happened to those of us who are Christ's or who have been born again? (I John 3:14)

   _____

4. What does Paul say has happened to him? (Gal. 2:20)

   _____

5. Paul said that Christ was living in him, that he lived only by the power of the Son of God. What enables us to share in this resurrection life and to be able to experience what Paul was talking about? (Rom. 6:5) As we have already seen, the opening ''for'' of Romans 6:5 takes us back to our baptism into Christ's death.
   a _____
   _____

   b What does this include? (Matt. 10:37-39; Luke 14:33)
      1. _____
      2. _____
      3. _____
   c In order for one to be raised from the dead, what must precede? (Rom. 6:2-4)

   _____

6. What things belong to our acceptance of God's way, wherein He promises to receive us? (II Cor. 6:14-18)
   a _____
   b _____
   c _____
   d _____

7. What then does God promise He will do for us? (II Cor. 6:17-18)

    a _____

    b _____

    c _____

8. Is there any way to be of the world and please God? (James 4:4)

    _____

9. Consequently we see that in order to share in Christ's life, we must also share in His death. After we submit ourselves to *death* with Christ, what does God promise? (II Tim. 2:11; Rom. 6:5,8)

    a _____

    b _____

    c _____

10. What are we who have died and risen with Christ to do with the "members" of our earthly bodies? (Col. 3:1-5)

    a _____

    _____

    How have believers "put off" the old man? (Col. 2:11-12)

    b _____

11. What is our position according to Colossians 3:3?

    a _____

    b _____

12. If we died with Him, what has happened? (Rom. 6:7,18)

    a _____

    b _____

13. Does sin have any power over us? (Rom. 6:14)

    _____

    _____

14. a How many times did Christ die to sin? (Rom. 6:9-10)

    _____

    b Can we die more than once? _____

    c Therefore is it not fallacy to think we have to constantly die to the sin nature? _____

15. a Consequently, what are we commanded to do? (Rom. 6:11)

    1. _____

    2. _____

    b How is this actually experienced?

    _____

16. How are we supposed to act according to Romans 6:13?

    _____

    _____

17. How do we walk in the Spirit, or walk in the resurrection life of Christ? (John 15:1-4)

    _____

18. Can a branch do anything of itself? (John 15:4)

_____

Can a branch bare fruit by striving, being anxious, by self-effort?

_____

19. How do we allow this divine life of Christ, this life-giving sap to flow through us? (Eph. 3:17)

_____

20. Through abiding in the vine, what actually happens? (Heb. 4:9-10)

a _____

b _____

21. Why do some who profess to know the Lord not experience the rest of abiding in the vine? (Heb. 3:18-19) Observe from Heb. 4:1-3 that those who experience real salvation do enter into that rest of faith.

_____

22. How does the branch abide with the vine? (John 15:7-13)

a _____

b _____

23. Whose life are we actually sharing? (Rom. 8:11)

_____

24. As we walk in the Spirit, whose life are we actually experiencing? (Col. 2:6)

_____

25. Why is this possible? (I Cor. 6:17)

_____

26. As we walk in the Spirit, what happens to our minds? (Rom. 12:2; I Cor. 2:16)

a _____

b _____

27. Consequently we are able to think God's thoughts.

a What are the best things to think on in order to keep our mind filled with God's thoughts? (Phil. 4:8)

1. _____ 3. _____ 5. _____
2. _____ 4. _____ 6. _____

b Where is the best place to find these things? _____

28. Can we expect to know God's thoughts? (I Cor. 2:9-10)

_____

29. What are two things we must do to have God's thoughts revealed to us? (Heb. 11:6)

a _____

b _____

30. As God's Word fills our mind, our conversation will be affected. What are three commandments concerning the conversation of Christians? (I Peter 4:11; II Tim. 2:16; James 3:2)

a _____

b _____

c _____

31. a As we walk in the Spirit, abiding and resting in the vine, what else can we look forward to experiencing? (John 15:11)

_____

b Will this joy be transient, will it come and go? _____

c How do we experience this joy? _____

32. a What did Christ pray in John 17:13?

_____

b Can we then expect anything less?

_____

33. a If we cease to experience joy, this is a sign that we are walking in the flesh, walking by our own effort and power. What is another sign that tells us we have stopped resting in the vine and are striving in our own efforts to walk in the Spirit? (I Cor. 3:3)

_____

b How do we get back into the Spirit? (I John 1:9)

_____

34. What is God's plan for those called according to His purpose? (Rom. 8:29)

_____

35. In anticipation of that day when His people will be finally transformed into Christ's image at the resurrection (see Rom. 8:29b), God provided certain ministries for His body. What are they? (Eph. 4:11)

a _____

b _____

c _____

d _____

e _____

36. What is the purpose of these ministries? (Eph. 4:12)

a _____

b _____

37. How long will these ministries be in operation? (Eph. 4:13)

a _____

b _____

c _____

d _____

38. When this happens the Church will fully exhibit Christ before the world in which it ministers. What will the world and the Lord notice about the Church? (Eph. 5:27)

_____

MEMORY VERSE: John 15:4

_____

_____

_____

_____

SERIES II

RIGHTEOUSNESS

*"Now that no one is justified by the Law
before God is evident;
for 'the righteous man shall live by faith.'
. . . For if a law had been given
which was able to impart life,
then righteousness would indeed have
been based on law."*

Galatians 3:11,21

*"That I may be found in Him, not having a righteousness
of my own derived from the Law,
But that which is through faith in Christ,
the righteousness which comes from God on the basis of faith."*

Philippians 3:9

SERIES II
RIGHTEOUSNESS
STUDY 1—THE RIGHTEOUSNESS OF GOD

The Bible says that **everyone has sinned.** Every person is under the same condemnation for "all have sinned." On the cross, Jesus took man's place. His soul was made an offering for sin, that sin should be *removed* from every soul who truly repents and accepts His forgiveness by *faith*. By *faith* that soul is cleansed in the Blood of Jesus. There is no need for another sacrifice and there is nothing you can add to your salvation to make it any more acceptable. It is not from man but from God. **The cross is where the new creation begins.** You come as a sinner, maybe in sickness and in poverty—and there you leave it all on the cross—on Jesus, who is *your* substitute. However, there are many saints of God who are going about trying to establish their own righteousness through their own works, striving to be in the *natural* what God says we are *naturally* in the Spirit.

1. Is there any sacrifice that we can offer to attain righteousness? (Heb. 10:1)

   _____

2. If there is no sacrifice we can make, or nothing we can do, how are we then "sanctified" or made holy? (Heb. 10:10)

   _____

3. How many times was this sacrifice made? (Heb. 10:10,14)

   _____

4. What is the one condition that is set forth as necessary to appropriate this righteousness in your life? (Gal. 3:22; Rom. 10:4,6a)

   _____

5. In what must you have faith or belief? (Rom. 3:22; Gal. 2:16; Heb. 9:12,22,26)

   _____

6. How then shall we be purged? (Heb. 9:13-14)

   _____

7. What is the one condition we must meet to have this blood applied to our sin? (I John 1:9)

   _____

   Is there anything we can do to be more worthy? _____

8. As a result, what two things will Christ do for us? (I John 1:9)

   a _____
   b _____

9. From what does He cleanse us? (I John 1:9)

   _____

   Therefore, how do we stand before God?

   _____

   Read Isaiah 6:1-8. This is an example of the righteousness that comes from God.

10. As a result of seeing the Lord, what did Isaiah realize? (Isa. 6:5)

   _____

11. What two things did Isaiah do when he saw his sin? (Isa. 6:5)

a _____

b _____

12. Because Isaiah was sorry for his sin, and confessed it, what did God do for him? (Isa. 6:6-7)

a _____

b _____

c What happened to his iniquity? _____

d Therefore, how did he stand before God? _____

13. Did Isaiah keep moaning and groaning before the Lord for forgiveness? Did he keep condemning himself? (Isa. 6:8)

_____

What did he do?

a _____

b _____

Is there anything he did to deserve this forgiveness?

_____

14. According to Jewish law, Isaiah was under the curse. Why? (Gal. 3:10)

_____

_____

15. Is any man justified by his own efforts or by the law? (Gal. 3:11)

_____

16. How then shall a man be justified? (Gal. 3:11-14)

_____

_____

17. Why was Isaiah as well as Abraham found worthy before God? (Gal. 3:6)

_____

18. Is there any law or group of laws that can bring righteousness or give life? (Gal. 3:21)

_____

19. Then what was the purpose of the law? (Gal. 3:19, 23-25)

a _____

b _____

20. How long was the law to guide? (Gal. 3:19)

_____

21. When the Seed came, that is Christ, what was established? (Heb. 8:7-12)

_____

22. a According to the New Covenant, what is our relationship to the law as we walk naturally by His Spirit? (Heb. 8:10)

_____

b As we walk in the Spirit, what should our new life *naturally* do?

_____

23. a According to the New Covenant what are we in Christ? (II Cor. 5:17)

_____

   b Are we a patched up "old man"?

_____

24. a What are we to do with the old man? (Eph. 4:22)

_____

   b How has it been put off? (Col. 2:11-12)

_____

   c How may we war against the old man when it opposes us in others? (II Cor. 10:4-5)
     1. _____
     2. _____
     3. _____

25. a What do we do with the new nature we have through Christ? (Eph. 4:24)

_____

   b How do we put on the new nature? (Eph. 4:23; Col. 3:10)
     1. _____
     2. _____

26. How is this new nature created? (Eph. 4:24)
     a _____
     b _____

As we walk by faith in what God has given us through Christ, what attitudes and moral qualities should our life naturally produce without any added effort on our part?

_____

27. What is the source of righteousness in our life? (Gal. 5:16)

_____

28. What does God say has actually happened to us? (Rom. 7:4-6)
     a _____
     b _____
     c _____

29. From what does God say you are naturally free? (Rom. 8:2)

_____

30. What are we to do to establish a right relationship with God? (Rom 3:21-22) Notice from verse 20 that Paul here speaks of "justification", that is, the being *counted as righteous* in God's sight—fully forgiven. On the basis of our being *counted* as righteous, the Spirit works *inward* righteousness in our hearts. Forgiveness thus is the basis of inward holiness.

_____

31. If we believe that there is power in the Blood of Jesus Christ and if we believe that God is able to do what He promises, then what can we expect? (Rom. 3:22; 6:14,22)
     a _____
     b _____
     c _____
     d _____
     e _____

32. In light of what we have learned from this study, how can we approach the throne of God? (Heb. 10:19,22)

a _____

b _____

c _____

d _____

MEMORY VERSE: Rom. 10:3-4

_____

_____

_____

_____

SERIES II
RIGHTEOUSNESS
STUDY 2—THE RIGHTEOUSNESS THAT IS BY FAITH

"For I am not ashamed of the gospel,
for it is the power of God for salvation
to everyone who believes . . .
For in it the righteousness of God
is revealed from faith to faith;
as it is written, 'but the righteous
man shall live by faith'"

Romans 1:16-17

* The Church has been very strong in teaching man his need of *righteousness*, his weakness and inability to please God. She has preached against unbelief, world conformity, and lack of faith, but she has been sadly lacking in bringing forward the truth of what we are in Christ, or how righteousness and faith are available.

Most of our hymns put our redemption off until after death:
- We are going to have rest when we get to heaven.
- We are going to have victory when we get to heaven.
- We are going to be overcomers when we get to heaven.
- We are going to have peace with God when we get to heaven.
- There will be no more failings when we get to heaven.

The hymns say we have nothing on this side except failure, misery, disappointment and weakness. What does the Lord mean when He says, "You are complete in Him, who is the head of all principality and power?" When are we to be complete? Is it in this life or in the next? What does He mean in Romans 8:37, "But in all these things we overwhelmingly conquer through Him who loved us." When are we to be more than conquerors? Is it after death when we leave this vale of tears? And Philippians 4:13 says, "I can do all things through Him who strengthens me." When is it that we are going to be able to do all things? Is it after we finish the course and stand with Him in the new heaven and the new earth? He declares in Romans 8:1, "There is therefore now no condemnation for those who are in Christ Jesus." When does this become ours?

When does Romans 5:1 become a reality? ("Therefore having been justified by faith, we have peace with God through our Lord Jesus Christ.") When are we to find this glorious thing called peace? When has Jesus "become to us wisdom from God, and righteousness and sanctification, and redemption"? Is that to come to us only at death, or is it a fact for us now? "He made Him who knew no sin to be sin on our behalf, that we might become the righteousness of God in Him." We know the first part is true. But is the last part true? Are we to become righteousness in the present life, or are we to become righteous after death?

The reason for practically every spiritual failure can be traced to sin consciousness. It destroys faith; it destroys the initiative in the heart. It gives man an inferiority complex; it robs us of all fellowship and communion with the Father.

I believe that what the Scripture says about us is absolutely true: that God Himself is now our very righteousness, and that we are the righteousness of God in Him. On the basis of this we are partakers of the divine nature (II Peter 1:4). There is no condemnation to us who "walk in the light as He Himself is in the light."

The whole teaching of the modern church in regard to separation from the world is vague and illusive. One branch of the church has taught that after we are born again we still have the "fallen nature" in us. That is the sin nature that came into Adam at the fall. Some men acknowledge the fact that God has provided a new birth but feel that His new birth is a flat failure. They think the only thing He can do is give us eternal life and forgive us, that He cannot give us victory over the old nature. This is not true because it is not the Word of God. II Corinthians 5:17, "Therefore if any man is in Christ he is a new creature; the old things passed away; behold, new things have come."

A man cannot be in Christ and be governed by the old nature. He is either in the family of God or in the family of Satan. I John 3:10 states, "By this the children of God and the children of the devil are obvious: anyone who does not practice righteousness is not of God, nor the one who does not love his brother." There can be no real development of faith, no strong, victorious Christian life with a mixed conception—we are either new creations or we are not. We have either passed out of death into life, or we have not. When Paul says, "Sin shall not lord it over you," he means exactly what he says. If you live a life of weakness and defeat it is because you do not know what you are in Christ. Until man is righteous and knows it, Satan reigns over him, and sin and disease are his masters. But the instant he knows that he is the righteousness of God in Christ and knows what that righteousness means, Satan is defeated. The supreme need of the Church at this hour is to know what we are in Christ, how the Father looks upon us, and what He considers us to be. *

1. The natural man is more than a sinner and violater of the law. What does II Corinthians 6:14 call him?

   a _____

   b _____

The natural man is iniquity, he is by nature a child of wrath. He is united with Satan as the believer is united with God.

2. When we were in the flesh, what was the *natural* fruit that we as children of the devil produced? (Rom. 6:19-21)

   a _____

   b _____

   c _____

Our lives in union with Satan naturally brought forth the fruit of iniquity. It flowed forth from us without effort.

3. What does this satanic nature produce in man? (Isa. 57:20-21)

   a _____

   b _____

   c _____

4. What has God done to deal with this satanic nature that is in man? (Col. 1:13-14)

   a _____

   b _____

   c _____

   d _____

We see from this that we have been delivered out of Satan's domain.

5. How did God accomplish this marvelous deliverance and why did Jesus become sin? (II Cor. 5:21)

   _____

   _____

Jesus was more than an offering for sin. He actually was made sin for our sin, and made unrighteousness for our unrighteousness. Christ sat down when His work was finished (Heb. 10:12). *Now* men can pass out of *death* and into *life*, they can become the righteousness of God in Him.

6. Whom does God justify? (Rom. 3:26)

   _____

7. Why was Christ manifested? (Heb. 9:26)

   _____

* Quotes are from Dr. E.W. Kenyan, *The Two Kinds of Righteousness*, chapter 1, page 6-8, by permission of Kenyan's Gospel Publishing Society, Inc.

8. How is the new man created? (Eph. 4:24)

a _____

b _____

9. What are all those who are in Christ? (II Cor. 5:17)

_____

What has happened to the old life?

_____

10. What else has happened to us? (Rom. 6:22)

a _____

b _____

c _____

d _____

Brethren, those who are going on to know the Lord, do we really believe all this? We can stand before God in this hour without *any* condemnation, sense of inferiority, guilt and unworthiness, and with absolute freedom. God has declared us to be all these things—to be righteous before Him, to be holy and without blame before Him. Jesus has paid a great price that we might know this righteousness. He says we are all these things.

11. What has the blood of Jesus done for us? (I John 1:7,9)

_____

12. How are we justified? (Rom. 5:1)

_____

13. How are we made righteous? (Rom. 3:20-22)

_____

14. How do we have access into this grace in which we stand before the throne of God without condemnation, sense of guilt, and free from inferiority, even the way Christ Jesus Himself stands before the Father? (Rom. 5:2)

_____

15. What has Jesus given us? (II Peter 1:3)

_____

16. To what has God called us? (II Peter 1:3)

_____

17. How are we made partakers of the divine nature? (II Peter 1:4)

_____

From what have we escaped? _____

18. The next few verses list the fruits of the Spirit. If we lack these fruits, what is wrong? (II Peter 1:9)

a _____

b _____

c _____

To stand before God with a sin consciousness robs us of fellowship with the Father. Because people are ignorant of the above Scriptures, they try to quiet their consciences by going to church, doing penance, fasting, giving money, saying prayers, doing good deeds, giving up pleasures, confessing sins, fighting bad habits, putting themselves under discipline of self-denial and self-abasement, by neglecting the body. All these methods have been tried. Every earnest spirit has attempted some of them.

19. If we seek to be justified by these things, what have we done? (Gal. 5:4; Gal. 2:21)

    a _____

    b _____

20. But what does the Word say? (Rom. 4:3,5)

    _____

21. Then, what can we conclude? (Rom. 4:16)

    _____

22. What does Rom. 8:1 say?

    _____

    Do we really believe this?

    _____

23. How are we to draw near the throne? (Heb. 10:22)

    a _____

    b _____

    c _____

    d _____

24. Do we dare to believe that we are what God says we are?

    _____

    If we do not, is God pleased? (Heb. 10:38)

    _____

We have become the righteousness of God in Him, but we have been living as slaves when we ought to reign as kings. We yielded without a fight when we heard the adversary roar about our unworthiness to stand in God's presence.

The sin problem stops being a problem the moment we know what we are in Christ's righteousness, and Sonship has ceased to be a problem when we know who the Word says we are.

Satan's dominion over us is broken. When you become a new creature, a partaker of the divine nature, the old nature loses its hold.

25. Whose children are we? (I John 3:2)

    _____

26. What has Jesus done for us? (Heb. 10:14)

    _____

27. What must we do in light of all these things? (Rom. 4:20-21)

a _____

b _____

c _____

d _____

And if we do these things, what do we now have? (Rom. 4:22-24)

_____

What are we exhorted to do? (Heb. 10:23)

_____

This new sense of righteousness, this new fact of righteousness, utterly destroys the sin consciousness, and we enter into that fellowship, the oneness with the Father against which the gates of hell cannot prevail.

MEMORY VERSE: Rom. 1:16-17

_____

_____

_____

_____

—NOTES—

SERIES II
RIGHTEOUSNESS
STUDY 3—NEW CREATION REALITY

"Jesus therefore was saying
to those Jews who had believed Him,
'If you abide in My word, then you
are truly disciples of Mine;
and you shall know the truth,
and the truth shall make you free.'"

John 8:31-32

Since the beginning of the New Covenant when God, through Christ, made it possible for man to become a new creature and to become born again of the spirit of God, Satan has been defeated. When the first person in the upper room became born again and filled with the Holy Spirit, Satan saw his slaves shaking off their manacles. He saw his prisoners set free. He saw joy-filled hearts where there had been tears; he saw the defeated become his master; he saw faith grow where doubt and fear had reigned. He saw a new race of men, a new species come into being. He saw the new birth take place. He saw God take men out of his grip and fill their hearts with love where selfishness had been. He saw men and women standing in the presence of God without a sense of guilt, inferiority, or condemnation. This shook the very foundations of hell.

Satan slew Jesus to destroy Him forever. Instead of that, His death and resurrection gave birth to this new creation family. They multiplied so rapidly that he realized he must destroy them before they destroyed him. Satan did not know this was going to be the result of his crucifying Christ. For Paul said in I Corinthians 2:7-8, "But we speak God's wisdom in a mystery, the hidden wisdom, which God predestined before the ages to our glory; which none of the rulers of this age has understood; for if they had understood it, they would not have crucified the Lord of glory."

Satan knew nothing of it. He saw he was defeated. Every time he destroyed a Christian, it gave birth to another. He feared God's Word on the lips of these new creation men more than anything he had ever faced. He tried to destroy the Word. Wherever God's Word was preached, it gave birth to new Christians. Satan saw these Christians fed on the Word, and in days they became more like the Master. To destroy the Word would stop their increase. During the 700 years of the Dark Ages, he tried to smother the Word, but Martin Luther gave birth to it again.

Even today Satan seeks to keep us from God's Word—and seeks to destroy the reputation and life of those who preach the truth that is found therein. It is imperative in these last days that we give God's Word its rightful place in our life, that we seek to understand it and that we by faith seek to walk in everything that God's Word says we are.

God has ordained that the generation of the end be one that walks in *everything* that God says that we are or can do.

"For as the earth brings forth its sprouts,
and as garden causes the things
sown in it to spring up;
So the Lord God will cause righteousness
and praise to spring up before all the nations.
For Zion's sake I will not keep silent,
and for Jerusalem's sake I will not keep quiet,
until her righteousness goes forth like brightness,
and her salvation like a torch that is burning.
A seed shall serve Him; it will be told
of the Lord to the coming generation."

Isaiah 61:11; 62:1; Psalm 22:30

Let us look now into that perfect law of liberty, that our minds might be enlightened to understand what we are in Christ that we might show forth the glory of Him who has called us from darkness to walk in this marvelous light.

1. How are we exhorted to live in this *present* age? (Titus 2:12)

   a _____

   b _____

2. Why did Christ give Himself for us? (Titus 2:14)

   a _____

   b _____

   c _____

3. Christ has redeemed us from all iniquity. What does the Bible say about us as the new creation? (Rom. 6:22; Col. 1:12-13; II Peter 1:3)

   a _____

   b _____

   c _____

   d _____

   e _____

   f _____

   g _____

We have been transferred from the kingdom of darkness into the kingdom of God. We are no longer governed by the old Adamic nature, but we are born by the Spirit of God; we are a new creature; we have not the nature of our old father Satan, but we have the nature of God our father, made possible through the sacrifice of Jesus.

4. In time past we found ourselves filled with sin, children of the darkness. How have we been created as a new creature? (Eph. 4:24)

   a _____

   b _____

5. If we as a new creature are created in righteousness and true holiness, and if we are not governed by the sin nature, then why do we react to certain things after the manner of the old life and sin against God? (Eph. 4:22-23)

   _____

It is because of the unregenerated, unrenewed mind, which is governed by the knowledge of the old life. We will go over some scriptures now that will explain this more fully, but first let us look at the drawing of the three types of men.

6. What is one thing that excluded us from the life of God? (Eph. 4:17-18)

   _____

7. Where were we enemies? (Col. 1:21)

   _____

The
Kingdom of Darkness

Facts About the Old Man:

1. Satan is the father of the old Adamic nature...

2. Bound by the sin nature...

3. Governed by the five senses...

4. Selfish nature...

5. Walking after the knowledge of this world...

6. Worldly, earthbound...

7. The wages of sin is death -- final destiny is hell...

Romans 6:23

The Kingdom of God

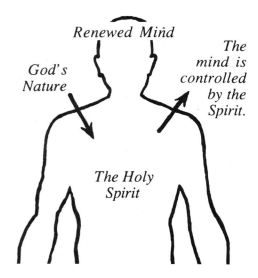

Carnal Mind

The spirit is imprisoned by the unrenewed mind.

God's Nature

The Holy Spirit

"Be transformed by the renewing of your mind."
Romans 12:2

Facts About the Spiritual Baby:

1. God is his Father...

2. Freed from the sin nature...

3. Because of ignorance is governed by the five senses...

4. Seeks his own way...

5. Walks after the knowledge of this world...

6. Worldly and earthbound through ignorance and unbelief...

7. Often defeated in this life...

Romans 8:6-8

Water baptism: Being baptized into Christ by faith
Burial of the sin nature, and rising with Christ by faith. (Galatians 3:26-27)

Blood line: The blood of Jesus His Son cleanses us from all sin. (I John 1:7)

Renewed Mind

God's Nature

The mind is controlled by the Spirit.

The Holy Spirit

Facts About the Spiritual Man:

1. God is his Father...

2. Freed from the sin nature...

3. Governed by the Word of God...

4. Love seeks not it's own...

5. Renewed in knowledge walking after the image of Jesus...

6. Through faith and patience inherits the promises...

7. Overcomes in all things, reigns as a king in this life...

Romans 5:17

8. What prayer did Paul pray for the early Christians in order that they might walk worthy of the Lord? (Col. 1:9-10; Eph. 1:17-19)

   a _____
   b _____
   c _____
   d _____
   e _____
   f _____
      1. _____
      2. _____
      3. _____

9. What does Paul exhort us to do? (Rom. 12:2)

   _____

10. How is the mind renewed? (Col. 3:10; John 15:3)

    a _____
    b _____

11. How does the type of life and godliness that we see recorded in the Bible become a reality in experience? (II Peter 1:3)

    _____

12. How are we made partakers of this divine nature? (II Peter 1:4)

    _____

13. How do we inherit these promises? (Heb. 6:12)

    a _____
    b _____

14. How then do we partake of the righteousness of God? (Rom. 9:30)

    _____

15. What kept Israel from experiencing righteousness? (Rom. 9:31-32)

    _____

Therefore, we see that in order to experience the new creation reality of righteousness (which means the ability to stand before God without guilt, inferiority, or condemnation), we must accept what God says we are *by faith* and *submit our mind to the Word,* that it might be renewed.

16. What will keep us from experiencing this reality of righteousness and godliness? (Heb. 4:1-3)

    _____

17. In James we see this teaching repeated again. What three things does he exhort us to do? (James 1:21-22)

    a _____
    b _____
    c _____

In James we are exhorted to lay aside all filthiness and all that remains of wickedness. We have already discovered that we have been made free from the old Adamic sin nature; consequently, this laying aside of wickedness has to do with the renewing of the mind that yet remains unrenewed.

Now the soul is the seat of our personality, intellect, and will. It is our mind area. As our mind is washed with the Word, we recognize those thoughts that are exalting themselves above the knowledge of the truth; therefore, we can cast these thoughts down. If we do not know what the Word says we are and can do, then we do not recognize the fiery darts of Satan.

18. In order to take the shield of faith (faith in the Word) to quench the fiery darts of the wicked one, what must we have first? (Eph. 6:14-16)

_____

What are the loins? (I Peter 1:13)

_____

We are exhorted in James to be doers of the Word and not hearers only. Faith requires action. If someone is sick, then we must be doers of the Word, laying hands on them that they may be healed. We must cast down every thought that tries to tell us it won't work and do it anyway.

19. If you have sinned, what should you do? (I John 1:9)

_____

According to this word, you are not only forgiven, but the problem is removed. There is no filthy thing dwelling within you. Your only need is to submit your mind to the Word, that it might be washed and renewed in whatever area of your life that you had the problem.

20. In order to be a doer of the Word, what must we do? (James 1:23-25)
    a _____
    b _____
    c _____
    d _____

Therefore, we look into the Word and believe what it says, not going our own way trying to remedy the problem, but accepting what God says we are and accepting His provision for us. We then act. This is being a doer of the Word.

21. James warns us not to be a forgetful hearer but to act on the Word we have received. Peter also exhorts us on this. In II Peter 1:5-8, the fruits of the spirit are listed. What reason does Peter give for lacking these fruits? (II Peter 1:9)
    a _____
    b _____

22. We see an example of Abraham's faith in the book of James. How did he demonstrate his faith? (James 2:21)

_____

23. What did Abraham believe? (Heb. 11:17-19)

_____

_____

24. How does faith come? (Rom. 10:17)

_____

_____

25. We find in Romans that there are two types of minds. What does it say about them? (Rom. 8:6)

a _____

b _____

26. What else is written about the mind set on the flesh? (Rom. 8:7)

a _____

b _____

c _____

To struggle then by our own works and efforts, by our trying harder, by our struggling to be more like Jesus, we will never come into His image, but will reap from the fleshly efforts death and condemnation.
Let us look again at our diagram of the three men.

27. Therefore, what the flesh, the law, and our own efforts cannot produce, God did. What did He do? (Rom. 8:3-4)

a _____

b _____

28. Are you under obligation to live according to the flesh, the carnal mind? (Rom. 8:12-13)

_____

29. Every false religion in the world is based on man's own efforts to attain to God and godliness. What is one difference between false religion that encourages man to produce good works by his own efforts and Christianity? (II Cor. 3:18)

_____

30. By what means does He give us the things that pertain to life and godliness? (II Peter 1:3)

_____

31. How do we find the knowledge of God? (Prov. 2:1-5)

a _____

b _____

c _____

d _____

e _____

f _____

g _____

32. When we find the knowledge of God, what will we then understand? (Prov. 2:9)

a _____

b _____

c _____

33. How is God's righteousness revealed to us? (Rom. 1:17)

_____

34. In the last days, the Spirit is being poured out. What is the end result of this going to produce? (Isa. 32:15-16)

a _____

b _____

35. What shall the work of righteousness produce and what shall the effect of it be? (Isa. 32:17)

a _____
b _____
c _____

36. What description do we have of the generation who will walk in God's righteousness? (Ps. 85:8-13)

a _____
b _____
c _____
d _____
e _____
f _____
g _____
h _____
i _____
j _____
k _____

—NOTES—

SERIES II
RIGHTEOUSNESS
STUDY 4—TAKING ON THE NATURE OF GOD

There is in the world today an abundance of moral sickness. There is the very fulness of Satan. It is apparent everywhere. Men are controlled by the devil. A new order is coming, however. Man is to be controlled by God, filled with His Spirit, His life, swayed by Him, ruled by Him.

1. For what purpose were we called? (Rom. 8:29)

   _____

2. God made the first man out of the dust of the earth. The first man is of the earth—earthy. From where is the "second man"? (I Cor. 15:47-49)

   _____

3. According to John, what is God's nature and how does this nature affect us? (I John 4:8)

   _____

4. How was the love of God manifested toward us? (I John 4:9)

   _____

5. How was true "agape" spiritually defined in Jesus? (I John 4:10; Rom. 5:7-8; Titus 3:3-7)
   a _____
   b _____
   c _____

6. What are we exhorted to do? (I John 4:11; John 15:9,13)
   a _____
   b _____
   c _____

7. How do we abide in the love of God? (John 15:10)

   _____

8. What is His commandment? (John 15:12)

   _____

9. If we keep this commandment, what will happen? (John 15:11)

   _____

10. How can we have this great love? (I John 4:7; Rom. 5:5)
    a _____
    b _____

We see from these verses that if we have been born again and filled with the Holy Spirit, we have received that love. It is like the measure of faith that we have received. We must exercise faith and love in order for it to grow in our heart. As we yield to love, selfishness stops reigning.

11. What are some ways in which we can exercise this love? (I Cor. 10:24; Rom. 15:1-2; I Cor. 10:33; Luke 6:27-28)

a _____

b _____

c _____

d _____

e _____

f _____

g _____

12. List the characteristics of this "agape" love that we have in our lives after we have been born of God. (I Cor. 13:4-7)

a _____ i _____

b _____ j _____

c _____ k _____

d _____ l _____

e _____ m _____

f _____ n _____

g _____ o _____

h _____

This is the supernatural love that is shed abroad in our hearts by the Holy Spirit. This love becomes strong by exercising it. Letting this love loose is letting God loose in you, for God is love. This love will lead a man out of selfishness, out of weakness and failure, into the very strength of Christ.

13. Is it possible for us to experience this kind of love? (Eph. 3:17-19)

_____

14. Knowing this love fills us with what? (Eph. 3:17-19)

_____

15. If we have been walking in love toward our family, friends, or enemies and they have not responded to God or they have treated us wrongly, what sure word of promise do we have? (I Cor. 13:8)

_____

16. As we believe in love and walk in the way of love what does this show about our relationship to the Father? (I John 4:16)

_____

17. As we walk in love, practicing it daily, what happens? (I John 4:17)

_____

—NOTES—

SERIES III

PRACTICAL CHRISTIAN LIVING

*"But the word is very near you,
in your mouth and in your heart,
that you may observe it."*

Deuteronomy 30:14

*Let the godly ones exult in glory;
Let them sing for joy on their beds.
Let the high praises of God be in their mouth,
And the two-edged sword in their hand.*

Psalm 149:5-6

SERIES III
PRACTICAL CHRISTIAN LIVING
STUDY 1—VICTORY IN THE HIGH PRAISES OF GOD

*"The weapons of our warfare are not of the flesh,
but divinely powerful for the destruction of fortresses.*

II Corinthians 10:4

There are many weapons in God's arsenal. One of the mightiest weapons is praise. This is more than just sincerely praising God, or even praising with an anointing. When one saint begins to praise the Lord, he can chase a thousand. But when the number of saints double, and two are joined together in their praises unto God, the results are multiplied ten-fold. For "Two shall put 10,000 to flight!"

And hear this, beloved . . . when a body of anointed saints of God begins to sound forth the high praises of God, devils tremble, the heavens are shaken, and thrones begin to topple. We are in a warfare, and God has put a mighty weapon into our hands. Humans living in a natural realm cannot understand the life of praise. But devils understand the language, and they hate it. For praise is the heavenly language of victory through Jesus. "Praising the Lord puts the devil to flight." It is the "high praises" of God that are to be in the mouth of His overcomer.

1. To what type of life are we called? (Eph. 5:18-20)

   _____

   How is this life of praise accomplished?

   a _____

   b _____

   c _____

   d _____

   e _____

2. Where does the power lie to continue walking in this *life* of praise and worship? (Eph. 5:18)

   _____

3. For what type of worshippers is God the Father looking? (John 4:23-24)

   _____

4. Why is praise so powerful? (Ps. 22:3)

   _____

Let us look at the record of previous saints, as examples for our learning, in the midst of battle. Read II Chronicles 20:12-23.

5. What did Jehoshaphat do when he saw his enemies were coming against him? (II Chron. 20:12)

   _____

6. If we apply the Lord's words to Judah, whose "battle" is it to deal with the things that come upon us? (II Chron. 20:15)

   _____

7. What were they exhorted to do? (II Chron. 20:17)

   a _____

   b _____

8. What position did God expect them to take? (II Chron. 20:20-21)

a _____

b _____

9. What happened to the enemy when the children of God began to sing and praise? (II Chron. 20:22-23)

_____

Read Numbers 14:22-30.

10. What kept the Israelites out of the promised land?

_____

11. Of what was this really a sign?

_____

12. What is the fate promised to Israel for not serving the Lord with a glad heart for the abundance of *all* things, that is being thankful for *all* things? (Deut. 28:47-48)

a _____

1. _____

2. _____

3. _____

4. _____

b _____

c _____

13. Jesus came to make it possible for us to rejoice. What provision did He make for us? (Isa. 61:3)

a _____

b _____

c _____

What does this joyful attitude of praise do for the Lord?

_____

14. Jesus was a man of sorrows and acquainted with grief. What was written about Him? (Heb. 1:9)

_____

15. In Christ's intercessory prayer, what did He pray for His own? (John 17:13)

_____

Christ has provided joy for us. Now! It is our inheritance. Child of God, if you lack joy, you must take it so this joy will be flowing through your life.

16. Psalm 137 speaks of the captivity of Zion which is like unto the Church which is in captivity to the doctrine of men and bound by tradition. What happened to Zion in captivity? (Ps. 137:1-4)

_____

17. What happened when Zion was brought forth from captivity? (Ps. 126:1-3)

a _____

b _____

c _____

18. The time for the restoration of all things is at hand. What is the characteristic of those people that will be a part of this restoration of Zion, the spiritual city of God? (Ps. 102:18-22)

_____

19. When the temple was restored under Hezekiah, what was the order of worship? (II Chron. 29:25-28)

_____

20. Jesus knew great joy through a life of praise and true worship of the Father. What is His desire now as He lives in His Church through the Spirit? (Heb. 2:11-12)

_____

21. Before any priest of the Old Testament could approach the Lord, he had to bring a sacrifice. What sacrifice ought we bring as New Testament priests? (Heb. 13:15)

a _____

How often are we to offer this sacrifice?

b _____

22. The Epistles teach us that we are living stones being built together as a holy habitation or house for the Lord. God is now in the process of restoring and building up this spiritual house. Read II Chronicles 5:11-14. What was the characteristic of the praisers and singers? (II Chron. 5:13)

_____

23. What did Jesus pray in His intercessory prayer that is being fulfilled? (John 17:20-23)

_____

24. What happened as they lifted up their voice to praise the Lord? (II Chron. 5:13-14)

a _____

b _____

25. What does Paul say shall happen to the saints in the last days? (II Thess. 1:10)

a _____

b _____

26. Read Psalm 149. In what type of people does the Lord take pleasure?

_____

27. How are we exhorted to praise the Lord? (Ps. 149:1-3)

a _____

b _____

c _____

d _____

28. What are we to do when we go to bed? (Ps. 149:5)

_____

29. We know that the overcomer is the one who rules and rejoices and executes judgment with Christ. What two things are characteristic of the Old Testament overcomer mentioned in Psalm 149:6?

a _____

b _____

30. What does the Psalmist say that the praise of God and the wielding of a two-edged sword will do? (Ps. 149:7-9)

a _____

b _____

c _____

d _____

e _____

How does this compare with what is written in Revelation 19:15 and Revelation 20:1-4?

_____

31. What are enemies the overcomer must conquer *now* with his "sword" of God's Word? (II Cor. 10:4-5)

_____

_____

Saints of God, press into God's best and highest. When we come together into worship and praise, let us not settle for just another service, just another time of fellowship. Let us press toward the mark for the prize of the high calling of God in Christ Jesus. Let us travail before God and believe God for a moving of His Spirit until from the time the worship service begins we will begin rising into the heavenly places with such a sound of victory and glory that devils will tremble, angels will shout and sing with us, and the voice of the Son of God will be heard in the midst of His Church!

—NOTES—

SERIES III
PRACTICAL CHRISTIAN LIVING
STUDY 2—THE LAW OF FAITH

In digging more and more deeply into this "law of faith", so that we might know and apply God's method in the performance of our God appointed task, we will discover a revelation in the Scripture by which God Himself performed His own first task of creation: and we are quick to realize that the same God indwelling us would use the *same eternal principles* in completing His New Creation.

We find the key to these principles in the Gospel of John. We who have been slaves to the visible world, things we can see and touch, make much of outward deeds and little of words. Yet what do we see in the principle of creation?

1. How were the worlds made? (Heb. 11:3)

_____

_____

2. Now what is faith? (Heb. 11:1)

_____

3. When God declared and said what would happen, what were the results? (Gen. 1:1-3,9,24)

_____

From this we see the principle of creation which in Hebrews 11:3 is called *faith.* "By *faith* we understand the worlds were prepared . . ."

4. What does this creative Word of God actually do? (Rom. 4:17)

_____

5. Is not this the same power that Christ has given unto us as the sons of God? What is written here? (Mark 11:22-24)

_____

_____

6. Let us look at the life of Christ. The Father thought His thoughts in Christ, for what did Jesus say? (John 12:49-50)

_____

7. What are we as believers exhorted to do concerning what and how to speak? (James 1:19; James 3:2; I Peter 4:11)

   a _____

   b _____

   c _____

   d _____

8. What lies in the power of the tongue? (Prov. 18:20-21)

_____

Man's responsibility lies in faith. Faith is two-fold. It is believing it in our heart and confessing it with our mouth.

9. What two exhortations are given to us concerning faith? (Heb. 10:23; I Tim. 6:12)

a _____

b _____

10. In order to fight the fight of faith what must we first do? (Heb. 11:13)

a _____

b _____

c _____

11. Having laid hold of the promises, the fight of faith begins. We may be assaulted and attacked by fiery darts of Satan. What will Satan try to do? (Gen. 3:1; John 9:44)

_____

12. When Abraham was thus tempted, what did he do? (Rom. 4:18-21)

a _____

b _____

c _____

d _____

e _____

f _____

13. As a result of the fight and labor of faith, what did Abraham receive? (Rom. 4:22)

_____

14. Was this written for Abraham's sake alone? (Rom. 4:23-24)

_____

15. What do those believers have need of who are fighting the good fight of faith but have not yet received the promise, or seen what they are believing for, come to pass? (Heb. 10:23,35-36)

a _____

b _____

16. If we do this, in whose steps will we follow? (Heb. 6:11-12)

_____

17. As we do believe God's Word, the Spirit of God will strengthen our faith so that we might have "full assurance of hope until the end" (Heb. 6:11). What will also be our experience? (Heb. 4:9-11)

_____

18. As we fight the good "fight of faith", for what shall we earnestly contend? (Jude 3)

_____

19. What were some examples of this faith? (Heb. 11:7,29,30) Also read verses 33-40.

a _____

b _____

c _____

20. Therefore, what are we exhorted to do? (Heb. 12:1-2)

a _____

b _____

c _____

21. What is the thing that will continue to make us victorious overcomers? (I John 5:4)

_____

—NOTES—

1. Because He has said, (Rom. 8:31)

_____

_____

we may boldly say, "God is for me and no one can succeed against me."

2. Because He has said, (III John 2)

_____

_____

we may boldly say, "God is concerned about the whole of my life."

3. Because He has said, (James 4:7)

_____

_____

we may boldly say, "The devil is fleeing from me, for I am steadfastly resisting him in Jesus' name."

4. Because He has said, (Luke 6:38)

_____

_____

we may boldly say, "The Lord is heaping up my blessings for I am giving to Him and to His work."

5. Because He has said, (Mark 16:18)

_____

_____

we may boldly say, when we lay hands on the sick, "They are recovering because I am acting on His Word."

6. Because He has said, (Mark 16:17)

_____

_____

we may boldly say, "Demons are going out because I have commanded them to go in Jesus' name."

7. Because He has said, (Ps. 91:14-16)

_____

_____

we may boldly say, "God is my deliverer in every case, because I love and serve Him."

8. Because He has said, (Ex. 14:14)

_____

_____

we may boldly say, "I know God is fighting for me because I am holding my peace: I have committed the battle to him."

9. Because He has said, (Isa. 65:24)

_____

_____

we may boldly say, "The Lord is answering my prayer even now as I pray; in fact, He was already working on the answer before I prayed."

10. Because He has said, (James 5:14-15)

_____

_____

we may boldly say, "The prayer of faith will heal me, and if I have committed any sins they will be forgiven."

11. Because He has said, (Heb. 13:18)

_____

_____

we may boldly say, "The word of God for the early church is God's word for me." (See verses 7 and 9)

12. Because He has said, (Matt. 8:13)

_____

_____

we may boldly say, "I can be on my way; I have prayed and believed; the answer will come."

13. Because He has said, (II Cor. 2:14)

_____

_____

we may boldly say, "I am always led in triumph and through me is manifested the sweet aroma of Him."

14. Because He has said, (Jer. 33:3)

_____

_____

we may boldly say, "The Lord is answering me and showing me great things because I am calling upon Him."

15. Because He has said, (John 15:11)

_____

_____

we may boldly say, "His joy is mine, and my joy is now full."

16. Because He has said, (Ps. 37:4)

_____

_____

we may boldly say, "The Lord grants me the desires of my heart, for I delight myself in Him."

17. Because He has said, (Acts 1:8)

_____

_____

we may boldly say, "I now have power for I have the Holy Spirit within."

18. Because He has said, (Rom. 8:1)

_____

_____

we may boldly say, "I have no condemnation, for I am in Christ."

19. Because He has said, (Ps. 84:11)

_____

_____

we may boldly say, "The Lord is withholding no good thing from me because I am walking upright before Him."

20. Because He has said, (John 15:7)

_____

_____

we may boldly say, "I am abiding in Christ, His words abide in me, and He is answering my wishes which are based upon His words."

21. Because He has said, (Matt. 5:8)

_____

_____

we may boldly say, "By His grace I shall see God, for the blood of Christ has made me pure in heart."

22. Because He has said, (I Peter 5:7)

_____

_____

we may boldly say, "I am carefree because all my cares are cast upon the Lord."

23. Because He has said, (Ps. 50:23)

_____

_____

we may boldly say, "I am glorifying my Creator by praising Him."

24. Because He has said, (John 16:24)

_____

_____

we may boldly say, "My joy is full because I am asking and receiving in Jesus' name."

25. Because He has said, (Isa. 26:3)

_____

_____

we may boldly say, "I have His perfect peace because my mind is steadfast and I trust in Him."

26. Because He has said, (Phil. 4:19)

_____

_____

we may boldly say, "I have every need supplied through His great riches toward me, as I give to His people." (Note verse 18)

27. Because He has said, (Mark 11:24)

_____

_____

we may boldly say, "I shall have my prayer request because I have prayed and have had faith for it; and I believe it is mine even now."

28. Because He has said, (Matt. 7:8)

_____

_____

we may boldly say, "I know I am receiving, because I have asked; 'everyone' means no exceptions—it includes me."

29. Because He has said, (Ps. 91:10)

_____

we may boldly say, "I am not afraid of disease nor evil; the Lord is my protection and health."

30. Because He has said, (Ps. 37:5)

_____

we may boldly say, "The Lord is working out every detail of my life, because I have committed it all to Him, and I am fully trusting Him."

—NOTES—

SERIES III
PRACTICAL CHRISTIAN LIVING
STUDY 4—DEVELOPING YOUR WALK IN THE SPIRIT

The secret of developing one's walk in the Spirit should be learned by every true Christian. You should make it your business to cultivate a sensitivity of your spirit to the wisdom and ways of the kingdom of God. The ability to allow God to use you significantly in His kingdom lies within you, but lies dormant until you act decisively upon His Word. This means dependence upon Him. There must grow in you the sense of His presence, a learning to depend upon Him, and an expectation that He will respond to you as you need Him and look to Him. This will result in your being sensitive to His Spirit.

You will discover His Word and Spirit transforming your faculties so that you will have a *Christian* mind, thinking God's thoughts after Him. You will learn to discern God's will in your spirit. You will learn to live more in the realm of the spirit, drawing upon the health and vigor that He gives to spirit, mind, and body. All this is available to you through meditation and assimilation of His Word. Let us stop wasting our time in foolish conversation and let us begin to utilize the potential God has given us and the opportunities that we have to study and act upon God's Word.

1. What picture does Paul give us of the unregenerated mind? (Eph. 4:17-18)
   a _____
   b _____
   c _____

Paul exhorts us not to walk in this type of mind. God has redeemed us out of this darkness. The moment that the spirit is recreated the mind may be renewed and brought into perfect harmony with the recreated spirit by the study of the Word. Wisdom is crying at the gate of our mind for entrance.
Read Proverbs 1:20-33.

2. In Proverbs we see a picture of Wisdom crying in the streets. She has made her feast. She is inviting you to come and join her. What two questions does Wisdom ask? (Prov. 1:22)
   a _____
   b _____

3. What admonishment and promises are we given? (Prov. 1:23)
   a _____
   b _____

4. If people have not sought after God's wisdom, the Scripture says that when destruction, fear and anguish come upon them and they try to seek wisdom, they won't find it. Why? (Prov. 1:29-30)
   a _____
   b _____
   c _____
   d _____

5. If we do hearken unto wisdom and seek it from above, what assurance do we have? (Prov. 1:33)
   a _____
   b _____

How the Father desires for us to have His wisdom dwelling within us! How He desires to have His Word fill our inward parts! How He longs for us to feast upon His Word, to sit and have fellowship with Him through His Word. He stands and cries at the gates of our minds and hearts for entrance. As we allow His Words to enter, we become transformed and changed into His image. Jesus longs to wash us in His Word. It is up to us to take the time to let His Words enter and dwell within us.
Read Proverbs 4:5-13.

6. What plea and exhortation is given to us in Proverbs 4:7?

a _____

b _____

7. What reward will we receive from doing this? (Prov. 4:8-10)

a _____

b _____

c _____

d _____

e _____

8. What other exhortation are we given in Proverbs 4:23?

_____

_____

This is the heart cry of the Father, for us to seek after wisdom and knowledge. Let us shake off the bonds of complacency and laziness and let us give place to God's Word in our life daily so that we can be changed into the likeness of our God and so hasten the coming of His kingdom. Wisdom is the Word of God. The Spirit will illuminate the Scripture and you will understand the mind of the Father.

9. What promises do we have from the Father concerning the Spirit of truth? (John 16:13-14)

a _____

b _____

c _____

(Jer. 33:3)

a _____

b _____

The Word of God that we hold in our hands was placed there through the blood of countless thousands of martyrs. For centuries during the Dark Ages the Bible was locked up in an unknown tongue and kept from men and women. Satan, through the guise of the Roman Catholic Church, said the Scriptures were too holy for the common man to read and so kept people in bondage to superstition and fear. As the Protestant Reformation began, men who had stumbled upon the Word of God and found the truth began translating the Bible in to the language of the people. The enemy, in the form of religious leaders of the day, began to wage war and kill the saints of God. During the Protestant Reformation, thousands upon thousands laid down their lives.

Early translators of the Bible died a martyr's death and countless thousands of men and women were burnt at the stakes for their testimony of Jesus and the Word of God. The blood of the martyrs was seed in the earth, and instead of the Bible being destroyed, the Word multiplied. After more than 1,000 years of darkness, the Word of God has been restored to us. We hold in our hand a book for which our brothers and sisters in Christ shed their blood, that we might read it and partake of its light and glory. Now Satan would try to keep us from this Word through worldliness, pleasure seeking, neglect, and self-satisfaction. He would seek to lull us to sleep through too much business and lack of meditation in God's Word. Let us not be slothful, but let us awake and seek the Lord.

10. What exhortation do the ungodly have from Isaiah? (Isa. 55:6)

_____

_____

11. In Proverbs 24 what is the description of a man who neglects the Word of God and the seeking of the Lord? (Prov. 24:30-31)

a _____

b _____

c _____

12. What was the reason for this desolation? (Prov. 24:32-34)

_____

This speaks to us of something greater than financial poverty, and that is spiritual poverty.

13. What exhortation do we have from Paul? (I Thess. 5:6-8)

a _____

b _____

c _____

d _____

14. What promise does Jesus give us? (John 14:21)

_____

_____

15. As we lift up the gates of our minds, to fill them with God's Word, how will Jesus manifest Himself to us? (Ps. 24:7-10)

_____

The manifestation is not one that the eye can feast upon, or the hands can touch, but it is a spiritual unveiling of the very heartlife of Jesus.

16. What instruction on studying the Word was Joshua given in Joshua 1:8, which we may apply to ourselves?

a _____

b _____

What will be the result?

a _____

b _____

In order to develop wisdom as it should be developed, it is going to be necessary that we have quiet hours of meditation in the Word. Meditate in Proverbs, the first ten chapters, and you will see the vast place that wisdom holds.

17. What exhortation does Paul give us concerning the Word? (Col. 3:16)

_____

18. What promise does Jesus give us if we let the Word abide in us? (John 15:7)

_____

As Christ's Word dwells richly in us, we will become more at one with Him. We will share more His attitudes and disposition (Colossians 3:12-15). We will share more His ability, His wisdom, and His authority (Colossians 3:17). Already we have the great and mighty Holy Spirit, who raised Christ from the dead, dwelling in us, energizing us. Thus, we can do Christ's works. There will grow between Him and us a friendship, as between two lovers, but a holy friendship in which we are ever eager to serve Christ as Lord.

19. Analyze Proverbs 3:5-6. What three things are we exhorted to do?

a _____

b _____

c _____

What will God then do? (Prov. 3:6)

d _____

Stop leaning on your own understanding. You have found Somebody who is wise. You are resting in Him. His ability has become your ability. His love has become your love. His strength has become your strength, and by His stripes you have found a perfect healing for spirit, soul, and body. You walk in the fulness of this wonderful heavenly union. His Word has become a part of you. You live in it. As you live and walk in His Word, His wisdom becomes yours.

20. As this Word and this wisdom dwell in us fully, what will be the fruit of our life? (James 3:17)
    a _____
    b _____
    c _____
    d _____
    e _____
    f _____
    g _____
    h _____

21. As we continue this love walk and seek God with all our hearts, what will be the result? (Eph. 3:16-19)
    a _____
    b _____
    c _____
    d _____
    e _____
    f _____

22. When God's people get filled with all the fulness of God, then what will be seen in the church? (Eph. 3:21; compare verses 19-20)

    _____

Let us, therefore, give ourselves to the study of God's Word. Let us redeem the time, let us stop wasting our time in foolish talk, in idle moments, and let us be filled with God's fulness. Let us let the Word of Christ richly indwell our lives so the glory of God might fill the Church and that the kingdom of God might be seen upon this earth as it is in heaven.

—NOTES—

SERIES IV

THE WORK OF THE MINISTRY

"Truly, truly I [Jesus] say to you,
he who believes in Me, the works that I do,
shall he do also; and greater works than these
shall he do; because I go to the Father."

John 14:12

"The Spirit of the Lord God is upon me,
because the Lord has anointed me to
bring good news to the afflicted;
He has sent me to bind up the brokenhearted,
to proclaim liberty to captives
and freedom to prisoners."

Isaiah 61:1

SERIES IV
THE WORK OF THE MINISTRY
STUDY 1—MINISTERING IN THE POWER OF THE SPIRIT

God's purpose for each Christian is to become an expression of God's will here upon this earth. That true purpose can only be to walk as the Lord walked, to show His love and power, to manifest His life. God has made it possible through Jesus Christ for every believer to become an effective minister. God has made it possible for you and me to be effective for the kingdom of God. God has given us the power of His Holy Spirit to carry out this objective. He puts within us—within you—His ability to fulfill His purpose for our lives on this earth right now. YOU DO NOT HAVE TO SIT AND WAIT.

You can be busy now and rejoice in it! You can be magnifying God and accomplishing something according to the plan of God, bringing to pass God's will upon the earth right now! In this study we will be discussing God's purpose for our lives and the greatness of His power toward us who believe.

1. What did Jesus call His twelve disciples to do? (Luke 9:1-2) Observe that power over demons and over disease (verse 1) attended the proclamation of the kingdom of God.

   _____

   Read Luke 4:40-44.

2. What did Jesus Himself preach when He walked the earth? (Luke 4:43)

   _____

3. What happened when Jesus preached the gospel of the kingdom? (Luke 4:40-41)
   a _____
   b _____

4. What was the commandment or commission that Christ gave unto His disciples? (Mark 16:15; Luke 24:47; Matt. 28:18-20)
   a _____
   b _____
   c _____
   d _____

5. What did Jesus tell His disciples to do before they went out to preach this gospel of the kingdom? (Luke 24:49)

   _____

6. What was supposed to happen to the disciples when they received this promise of the Holy Spirit? (Acts 1:8)

   _____

7. When Jesus first began His ministry, He received the empowering, the anointing of the Holy Spirit. For what did Christ say that the Spirit has anointed Him? (Luke 4:18-19)
   a _____
   b _____
   c _____
   d _____
   e _____

8. Do we have the same Holy Spirit that Jesus had? (Gal. 4:6)

   _____

9. What did Jesus say He came to do? (Matt. 20:28)

a _____

b _____

10. If you want to be great in the kingdom of God, what did Jesus say for you to do? (Matt. 20:26-27; Matt. 5:19)

a _____

b _____

c _____

d _____

11. Where is the place of greater blessing than in receiving to be found? (Acts 20:35)

_____

12. What command is given to us by Peter? (I Peter 4:10-11)

_____

13. How did Paul view his ministry? (II Cor. 3:6) Note: Paul was speaking of the ministry that he and Timothy had to others, particularly to the Corinthians in this case (see II Corinthians 1:1). Today those whom God calls have a ministry similar to that of Paul. In one sense we should all be ready to proclaim the Word and thus extend the ministry of the Apostle Paul (cf. I Peter 3:15).

_____

What characterizes the "new covenant"? (II Cor. 3:6)

_____

14. Of what kind of ministry are we speaking? (II Cor. 3:7-11)

_____

15. Since we have such a hope within us, and such a glory within us, how should we minister this "Life"? (II Cor. 3:12-18)

a _____

b _____

16. Seeing that we have this ministry, what does Paul exhort us to do? (II Cor. 4:1)

_____

17. What is that "Spirit" that we are ministering? (II Cor. 3:17; Rom. 8:11)

a _____

b _____

18. Ought we to preach *our* virtues, or *our* power, etc.? (II Cor. 4:5,7)

a _____

b _____

19. What did God promise to Israel concerning a ministry to the needy? (Isa. 58:10,11)

a _____

b _____

c _____

d _____

e _____

f _____

g _____

We are called not to minister "ourselves", but to proclaim the risen Lord, and thus to work toward bringing the world into harmony with God's will. Let us now see what we *have* received in Christ; let us look into the greatness of His power toward us who believe.

20. Do we lack anything with Christ as our life? (Col. 2:9-10)

   _____

21. What have we received from Him? (John 1:16; I Cor. 2:16)

   a _____

   b _____

   c _____

Through our experience of the grace and mind of Christ, we come to experience the character and ability of Christ. The character of Christ is resident in the fruit of the Spirit; the ability of Christ is resident in the gifts of the Spirit. The character of Christ is ours to minister unto others.

22. What are the nine fruits that reside in us as believers? (Gal. 5:22,23)

   a _____   f _____

   b _____   g _____

   c _____   h _____

   d _____   i _____

   e _____

If we know that Christ is in us through His Spirit, then we can appropriate this fruit. We can also pray for others and encourage them to allow this expression of the Spirit in their lives.

23. In ministering through the Spirit to others, what "virtue" would you encourage in the following people:

   Problem   *Virtue*

   a. unloving   _____

   b. the nervous, fearful, frustrated   _____

   c. the sad and despondent   _____

   d. the anxious and impatient   _____

   e. the rude and insensitive   _____

   f. the arrogant, crude, and undeserving   _____

   g. the unbelieving, doubting person   _____

   h. the haughty and proud   _____

   i. the hasty, unthinking   _____

God allows these types of people to come into your life so that Christ can function through you to minister life to them. Never agree with the persons who have the above problems, and never argue with them. Instead, recognize this as a chance to let Christ minister through you HIS virtue in a needy world.

—NOTES—

SERIES IV
THE WORK OF THE MINISTRY
STUDY 2—MINISTERING IN THE POWER OF THE HOLY SPIRIT

Jesus said, "The works that I do, shall he do also; and greater works than these shall he do; because I go to the Father" (John 14:12). It was, and is, God's determined will that the members of the Church, which is the Body of Christ, shall do the same works Jesus did in His own body, and that toward the end of this age, these works shall be greater, which we believe means greater in number, spreading all over the world before Jesus returns.

Christ means "the Anointed One". History records that Jesus received this anointing after He was baptized in water by the coming of the Spirit in the shape of a dove, lighting on Him. If we are to take our places in the Body of the Anointed One, surely we need to have a similar anointing. The Holy Spirit enables the believer to manifest the nature of God in the operation of the gifts of the Spirit. The Spirit uses these gifts to manifest the power of Jesus to the world through the believer.

As there are seven compounded colors in white light, with infrared on one side of the spectrum and ultraviolet on the other, so are the nine gifts of the Spirit. These nine gifts are the very essence of the Holy Spirit and do not exist apart from Him. The seven colors which together make up white light that we get from the sun may be used as an analogy of the nine gifts of the Holy Spirit which are all in the Holy Spirit. When a person receives the baptism of the Holy Spirit, he also receives potentially all nine gifts.

The Lord in His knowledge stirs us up to desire certain gifts, and as we exercise the necessary faith, the particular gift or gifts will begin to operate through our lives, not automatically, but only through our personal faith.

1. What are nine gifts of the Spirit? (I Cor. 12:4-11)

   a _____   f _____
   b _____   g _____
   c _____   h _____
   d _____   i _____
   e _____

2. These gifts can be divided into groups of three. Though all nine gifts are interrelated, it seems that these work in close teams with each other. What are the three oral gifts?

   a _____
   b _____
   c _____

   What are the three revelation gifts?

   a _____
   b _____
   c _____

   What are the three power (action) gifts?

   a _____
   b _____
   c _____

3. For what is this manifestation of the Spirit given? (I Cor. 12:7)

   _____

4. Do these gifts exist apart from the Holy Spirit? (I Cor. 12:4)

   _____

5. We are told in Scripture to seek spiritual gifts. If we have received the baptism of the Holy Spirit, and are daily filled with the Spirit, all nine gifts are potentially resident in us. What does Paul tell us to do? (I Cor. 14:1)

a _____

b _____

6. The word in the Greek New Testament for *gifts* in I Corinthians 12:4 is a form of *charismata* (plural). When one receives the gift (*dorea*, Greek) of the Holy Spirit (for example Acts 2:38), one has these *charismata* (gifts of grace). The word used for "gift" in the Greek in II Timothy 1:6 is *charisma* (singular). In this case, what is Paul exhorting Timothy to do? (II Tim. 1:6)

_____

7. Why do we have prophecy? (I Cor. 14:4)

_____

8. What does Paul desire for us to do in regard to prophesying? (I Cor. 14:5)

_____

9. What three things does prophecy do? (I Cor. 14:3)

a _____

b _____

c _____

Prophecy never reproves or rebukes. We have the written Word of God for this. Prophecy never contradicts Scripture.

10. If an unbeliever comes into an assembly and all people there are prophesying, what will happen? (I Cor. 14:24-25)

a _____

b _____

c _____

d _____

e _____

11. If we have the testimony of Jesus Christ, what do we have? (Rev. 19:10)

_____

In Revelation the *testimony* of Christ means the confession of Jesus, which comes from an inward conviction of one who is willing to lay down his life for this testimony (see Rev. 6:9; 12:11; 20:4).

12. The word *prophecy* in the original Hebrew can mean *bubble up* as from a spring. What does Jesus say in John 7:38-39?

_____

_____

This bubbling up (prophecy) of the living Word of God will come forth as a stream of life invigorating everything it touches. The living Word creates life. The word "prophecy" therefore has a larger connotation than just the gift of prophecy. It is the creative Word which dwells in us.

13. What is the power of this Word that dwells within us? (Heb. 11:3)

_____

14. We see Elijah practicing this same power. What did he do in I Kings 17:21-22?

_____

What did Elijah do in II Kings 2:8?

_____

_____

15. These were just a few of the things Elijah did by the creative Word that was in him. Elisha, who succeeded Elijah, did even greater things. What happened in II Kings 4:42-44?

_____

What did he do in II Kings 5:6,14?

_____

16. When Elisha died, he was so full of the creative Word of God what miracle happened after his death? (II Kings 13:20-21)

_____

The Spirit of the Lord today must move in and through the Church and lift up a standard of the Word of God through which Satan cannot penetrate and which will stop him in his tracks. We must rise up and take the authority which God has given us and *enforce* the victory of Calvary over the world, the flesh, and the devil.

—NOTES—

SERIES IV
THE WORK OF THE MINISTRY
STUDY 3—SETTING THE CAPTIVES FREE

Over one third of Jesus' ministry was in the area of deliverance. In Luke 4:18 it is written of Jesus,

"The Spirit of the Lord is upon Me,
Because He anointed Me to preach the gospel to the poor.
He has sent Me to proclaim release to the captives,
And recovery of sight to the blind,
To set free those who are downtrodden."

This is the ministry that Jesus gave the Church. He declared in John 14:12 that we are to do the same works that He did. Everywhere that Jesus went, He set the captives free. It is now time for the true believers to come forth and take dominion over satanic invasions in this world. Much of the sickness, abnormal attitudes, nervousness, poverty, fear, etc., are satanic forces turned loose upon the individual.

The world is filled with problems which are nothing but demon spirits taking over. The world needs our help. The Scripture warns us about increased demon activity in the end times, so we must be sober, diligent, and guard our own souls as well as others. Woe to the slothful minister in this day. Stop turning a deaf ear to the needs of the flock. Shake yourself from the dust of tradition and arise in the very ministry of Jesus Christ.

Isaiah 52:1-2 tells us, "Awake, awake, clothe yourself in strength . . . shake yourself from the dust, rise up, . . . loose yourself from the chains around your neck, O captive daughter of Zion." This is God's Word for you today. God is exhorting us to take the authority that is already ours and to defeat the works of the enemy. This is the role of the overcomers.

1. What happens to a person who continually yields to a particular sin or is overcome in a certain area? (Rom. 6:16; II Peter 2:19)

   a _____

   b _____

2. What else will bring us into bondage? (I John 2:15-16)

   a _____

   b _____

   What is in the world?

   1. _____

   2. _____

   3. _____

3. Rebellion is equal to what sin? (I Sam. 15:23)

   _____

   Insubordination is equal to what sin?

   _____

4. Sometimes people can be held in bondage by abnormal attitudes that are handed down through the family. Why does this sometimes happen? (Deut. 5:9)

   _____

   _____

5. To a person who is unfairly or constantly critical of others, what does God promise? (Ps. 101:5; Matt. 7:1-2)

   a _____

   b _____

   c _____

6. Worrying is another thing that causes us to be in rebellion to the written Word of God. Worry brings premature death and sickness. Instead of giving place to worry, what does the Word of God exhort us to do? (Ps. 37:5)

a _____

b _____

If we do this what is guaranteed to happen?

c _____

7. There are two mental attitudes that we can yield to that are in direct rebellion to the Word and will bring us into captivity. What are they?

a (Prov. 24:30-34)

_____

God equates the sluggard with what type of person? (Prov. 24:30)

1. _____

b (Ex. 31:12-17)

_____

What did the Lord promise to those in Israel who would keep one day of rest? (Isa. 58:13-14)

1. _____

2. _____

8. Our speech is very important in our life of victory over sin and the devil. What does Jesus say about this? (Matt. 12:37)

a _____

b _____

What else does the tongue bring upon us? (Prov. 12:13-18; Prov. 13:3; Prov. 15:4)

a (v.13) _____

b (v.13) _____

c (v.14) _____

d (v.18) _____

e (v.3) _____

f (v.3) _____

g (v.4) _____

h (v.4) _____

9. What is another way that darkness can grip our soul? (I John 2:9-10)

_____

In order to get deliverance for ourselves and others there are several conditions that must be met.

10. What must we do about sin? (John 5:14)

_____

11. If a man repents and gets delivered and yields again to the force of darkness, what will happen? (Luke 11:24-26)

_____

_____

12. Those seeking deliverance must cease from walking in hate, revenge, and critical or negative spirits. In what does the Scripture admonish us to walk? (Col. 3:14; Prov. 10:12)

_____

13. What else does Jesus require of those seeking forgiveness? (Matt. 6:14-15)

_____

14. Some demons have a legal right to be in a person. Why? If we will not forgive, what will happen to us? (Matt. 18:23-35)

_____

_____

15. James exhorts those seeking healing. What does he say is necessary? (James 5:16)

_____

If we do confess our sins, of what are we assured? (I John 1:9)

a _____

b _____

16. We must avail ourselves to the cleansing agent—the blood of Jesus. Satan hates the blood of Jesus. How is Satan overcome? (Rev. 12:11)

a _____

b _____

c _____

17. After deliverance what must we do in order to have constant cleansing of the blood of Jesus available? (I John 1:7)

_____

18. In order to stay delivered what must we do? (John 14:23)

_____

19. We must also continue to walk in that wisdom from above. James 3:14-18 tells us of two types of wisdom. One is a breeding ground for demonic activity—the other is a fertile field to produce righteousness. What are the characteristics of this earthly wisdom that we must resist? (James 3:14-16)

a _____

b _____

c _____

d _____

In what wisdom must the servant of the Lord seek to operate? (James 3:17-18)

a _____   e _____

b _____   f _____

c _____   g _____

d _____   h _____

20. The delivered saint of God must walk in a spirit of worship and victory. How can this type of spirit be developed? (Eph. 5:18-20) See also Ps. 34:1.

a _____

b _____

c _____

21. Who has the authority over demons? (Luke 9:1; Luke 10:19; Mark 16:17; John 14:12)

_____

22. Do unbelievers have power over demons? (Acts 19:13-17)

_____

23. On Jesus' first tour of Galilee, where did He first minister deliverance? (Mark 1:21-26)

_____

24. What did they say about the deliverance ministry of Jesus? (Mark 1:27)

_____

25. What were some of the manifestations of this particular demon? (Mark 1:24,26)
    a _____
    b _____
    c _____

26. What did the religious leaders say about Jesus' deliverance ministry? (Matt. 12:24)

_____

27. What did Jesus say about their accusation? (Matt. 12:25-26)

_____

_____

28. Of what did Jesus say that His casting out of demons, if by the Spirit of God, was a sign? (Matt. 12:28)

_____

29. Did the New Testament Church deal with deliverance? (Acts 8:7; Acts 19:11-12)

_____

30. What is one way of discerning an evil spirit? (Luke 11:34-36)

_____

31. What sure word of promise do we have from Jesus? (Matt. 16:18-19)

_____

Here is a list of verses to stand on when casting out demons: Col. 1:12-13; Col. 2:15; I John 4:4; James 4:7; Eph. 6:10-12; Luke 4:18; Luke 10:19; II Tim. 1:7.

"So they will fear the name of the Lord
from the west and His glory
from the rising of the sun,
For He will come like a rushing stream,
Which the wind of the Lord drives.
And a Redeemer will come to Zion,
and to those who turn from transgression in Jacob.
Arise, shine; for your light has come,
and the glory of the Lord has risen upon you.
For behold, darkness will cover the earth,
deep darkness the peoples;
But the Lord will rise upon you,
and His glory will appear upon you."

Isaiah 59:19-21;60:1-2

—NOTES—

SERIES IV
THE WORK OF THE MINISTRY
STUDY 4—A STUDY OF YOUR RESPONSIBILITIES AS A MINISTER OF THE "GOOD NEWS" OF JESUS

1. What is our commission as disciples of Jesus? (Matt. 28:19)

   a _____

   b _____

   c _____

This is the responsibility and privilege of the Church, of which every Christian is a part. This is the method that God has chosen to fill the whole earth with His glory.

2. Jesus was the Word made flesh. When people beheld Him, what did they see? (John 1:14)

   _____

Jesus was the "living Word". As men looked upon Him, they beheld God's glory. We too are begotten sons of God, born again by the Word of truth. As the Word of God dwells in us richly, men will behold God's glory. As we disciple others, teaching them how to live and walk in the truth of the Word, the earth will begin to be filled with God's glory.

3. What command do we have from Jesus? (Matt. 10:27-28)

   _____

4. If we seek to please men, from what role are we disqualified? (Gal. 1:10)

   _____

5. What was the prophet exhorted to do in Isaiah 58:1?

   a _____

   b _____

   c _____

   d _____

6. In order to direct people correctly and turn them from the evil of their way, what must prophets do? (Jer. 23:21-22)

   _____

7. What is the best way for us to stand in the Lord's council? (Ps. 15)

   a _____

   b _____

   c _____

   d _____

   e _____

   f _____

   g _____

   h _____

8. In Ezekiel's prophecy what were the Levitical priests to teach the people? (Ezk. 44:23, see verse 15)

   a _____

   b _____

9. By learning from the example of God's command to Jeremiah, what will we be careful to do when speaking God's Word? (Jer. 26:2)

_____

10. What exhortation did God give to Jeremiah concerning the fear of men? (Jer. 1:7-8,17)

a _____

b _____

c _____

11. What exhortation did God give to Ezekiel concerning the fear of men? (Ezk. 2:6-8)

a _____

b _____

c _____

12. As both Jeremiah and Ezekiel were commissioned to speak the words of God, what did God promise them? (Jer. 1:18-19; Ezk. 3:8-9)

a _____

b _____

c _____

d _____

e _____

f _____

13. What did Jeremiah say that one who had a dream from God or a word from God was to do? (Jer. 23:28) Note: In this passage Jeremiah is warning against false dreams and false prophecies (verses 25-27,32), and he is concerned that only the true word of the Lord be spoken.

a _____

b _____

14. As the true prophets in Jeremiah's day would speak God's word of judgment upon Judah (see Jeremiah 23:19-22 and also 1:1-19), what would this word be like? (Jer. 23:29) Note: When we speak similar words from the Lord in faith, we can expect the word to have a similar effect.

a _____

b _____

15. What practices is God against in so-called prophets? (Jer. 23:30-32)

a _____

b _____

c _____

16. In order to avoid such errors, what are we to do? (II Tim. 2:15-16,22-25)

a _____

b _____

c _____

d _____

e _____

f _____

g _____

17. What are we to do in order to maintain pure devotion in the Lord's service? (II Tim. 2:3-5)

a _____

b _____

c _____

—NOTES—

SERIES IV
THE WORK OF THE MINISTRY
STUDY 5—THE CHARACTER AND QUALIFICATIONS OF
MINISTERING THE GOSPEL

1. When Jesus called His disciples to follow Him, how did they respond? (Matt. 4:18-22; Matt. 9:9)

   _____

2. In the parable of the marriage feast, what disqualified those who were invited? (Matt. 22:1-14, especially v. 5)

   _____

   _____

3. With what statement does this parable close? (Matt. 22:14)

   _____

4. What are the qualifications of those that are with the Lamb? (Rev. 14:4-5; Rev. 17:14)

   a _____

   b _____

   c _____

   d _____

   e _____

5. What are the qualifications of one who would be great in the kingdom of God? (Matt. 20:25-28)

   a _____

   b _____

6. What quality of dedication do we see in Paul's life that made him so great a minister? (Acts 20:22-29)

   a (v. 24) _____

   b (v. 24) _____

   c (v. 27) _____

7. What other qualities do we see in the lives of Paul and other apostles of the early church? (I Cor. 4:9-13)

   a (v. 10) _____

   b (v. 11) _____

   c (v. 12) _____

   d (v. 12) _____

   e (v. 12) _____

   f (v. 13) _____

   g (v. 13) _____

8. How did these early Christians prove their ministries? (II Cor. 6:3-10, especially v. 3-4)

   _____

   _____

9. How did they present their message? (I Thess. 2:3-11)

a (v. 3) _____

b (v. 4) _____

c (v. 5) _____

d (v. 6) _____

e (v. 7) _____

f (v. 8) _____

g (v. 9) _____

h (v. 10) _____

i (v. 11) _____

10. The word "minister" means a servant. As we are entrusted with the good news of Jesus, what descriptive titles are we given in the Scripture? These titles are descriptive of the work as well as the character of those to whom the gospel is committed.

a   II Cor. 5:20 _____

b   Rev. 1:20, 2:1 _____

c   Matt. 4:19 _____

d   Phil. 1:7 _____

e   I Thess. 3:2; II Cor. 6:1 _____

f   John 5:35 _____

g   Deut. 33:1 _____

h   Mal. 2:7 _____

i   Isa. 61:6 _____

j   Ezk. 45:4 _____

k   II Cor. 11:15; II Peter 2:5 _____

l   Phil. 2:25 _____

m   Rev. 1:20; 2:1; Dan. 12:3 _____

n   I Peter 4:10 _____

o   I Cor. 4:1 _____

—NOTES—

SERIES IV
THE WORK OF THE MINISTRY
STUDY 6—THE IMPORTANCE OF BEING SENSITIVE TO PEOPLE'S NEEDS

When Jesus read from the prophet Isaiah in the synagogue, He read Isaiah 61:1-2. The rest of the chapter (and chapter 62) contains an Old Testament picture of the glories of the age to come, when Christ's kingdom will finally triumph. But in the church, the dawn of that future triumph has already arrived. Let us analyze portions of this passage to see what our ministry is to the world and to the Body of Christ.

1. By what name are we called? (Isa. 61:6)

    a _____

    b _____

2. What is the messianic ministry in which we now have a part? (Isa. 61:2-3)

    a _____

    b _____

    c _____

    d _____

3. When we begin to minister to people individually and personally in these areas of need, figuratively, what will then begin to happen? (Isa. 61:4)

    a _____

    b _____

    c _____

    d _____

So we see then in order for restoration to take place we must be concerned for the individual needs of the body members and unbelievers, to help them rise above their circumstances, get the victory, and overcome.

When we begin to be sensitive to the needs of others and to minister to them in this way, the ruins of the Body of Christ will begin to be rebuilt and repaired. This type of ministry takes a real laying down of your life, your desires, and what is convenient for you, to help and minister to someone else.

4. What is this type of laying down your life for another called? (Rom. 12:10)

    a _____

    b _____

5. As we are willing to lay down our lives and look after the needs of others, in the language of Isaiah, we are placed as watchmen in the city of God. What then is our responsibility? (Isa. 62:6-7)

    a _____

    b _____

    c _____

    _____

6. What else are we to do? (Isa. 62:10)

    a _____

    b _____

    c _____

    d _____

    e _____

7. What specifically is the duty of the watchmen? (Ezk. 33:1-7)

_____

8. If the people do not heed the warning, who is held responsible? (Ezk. 33:3-4)

_____

9. If the watchman sees the problem and does not confront the people with it, who then is responsible if the people fall away? (Ezk. 33:6)

_____

According to the book, *Manners and Customs in the Bible,* the passage refers to the duties of a certain officer of the temple called "the ruler of the mountain of the house". He went about the temple at every watch with lighted torches to see whether or not the guards were at their posts. If he found one of them sleeping, he struck him with a stick and burnt his garments. When it was said by others, "What is that noise in the court?" the answer was made, "It is the noise of a Levite under correction and whose garments are burning because he slept upon the watch."

It was also the custom in Bible times for the gates of walled towns to be shut at sundown. Travelers often hastened in their journey when they saw the sun setting to reach the city gates before they closed. If they were too late, they were compelled to spend the night outside exposed to storms and robbers.

10. The redeemed people of God are also represented as a walled city. When are her gates shut? (Isa. 60:11)

_____

11. How do we show the love of God toward others? (I John 3:16-18)
    a _____
    b _____
    c _____

12. What example did Jesus leave for us to follow? (Mark 10:42-45)

_____

13. For those who give themselves to this, what shall they receive? (Isa. 61:7-8, see "ministers" in verse 6)
    a _____
    b _____
    c _____
    d _____

14. As what will the world recognize them? (Isa. 61:9)

_____

—NOTES—

ANSWERS

"I directed my mind to know, to investigate, and to seek wisdom and an explanation. . . ."

Ecclesiastes 7:25

SERIES I
BROKENNESS
STUDY 1—THE PATH OF THE CROSS

Correct Answers

Question No.	Answers

1. You must bear your cross and come after Him.
2. a. We must lose our life for His sake in order to find it.
   b. To live is Christ, and to die is gain.
3. a. Present your bodies a living sacrifice.
   b. Be not conformed to this world.
   c. Be transformed by the renewing of your mind.
4. a. He emptied Himself (became of no reputation).
   b. Took upon Himself the form of a bond-servant.
   c. Humbled Himself.
   d. Became obedient unto death.
5. We have become united with Him in the likeness of His death.
6. He who falls into the earth and dies.
7. a. If we died with Him, we shall also live with Him.
   b. If we endure, we shall also reign with Him.
8. Baptism of fire.
9. a. Like a refiner's fire.
   b. Like fullers' soap.
   c. Like a smelter and purifier of silver.
10. a. Purify them.
    b. Refine them as gold and silver.
11. That they may present to the Lord offerings in righteousness.
12. a. Are you able to drink the cup that I am about to drink?
    b. Are you able to be baptized with the baptism with which I am baptized?
13. To do the will of the Father.
14. He despised the shame, but endured for the joy that was set before Him.
15. a. Refused to be called the son of Pharaoh's daughter.
    b. Chose to endure ill-treatment with the people of God.
    c. Considered the reproach of Christ greater riches, for he looked to the reward.

SERIES I
BROKENNESS
STUDY 2—THE ENDURANCE OF PERSONAL TRIALS

Correct Answers

Question No.	Answers

1. a. Produces endurance.
   b. That you may be perfect and complete.
   c. That you may be lacking in nothing.
2. a. Consider it all joy.
   b. Let endurance have its perfect work.
3. The crown of life.
4. a. They are for a season.
   b. Cause you to be distressed.
   c. They are various.
5. Greatly rejoice.
6. More precious than gold.
7. a. That we may be found to result in praise and glory and honor at the revelation of Jesus.
   b. That you may be considered worthy of the kingdom of God.
8. They were burdened excessively and despaired even of life.
9. That they would not trust in themselves, but in God.
10. The light of the knowledge of the glory of God.
11. a. Afflicted in every way, but not crushed.
    b. Perplexed, but not despairing.
    c. Persecuted, but not forsaken.
    d. Struck down, but not destroyed.
12. Carrying about in the body the dying of Jesus.
13. That the life of Jesus may be made manifest in us.

Correct Answers

Question No.	Answers

1. a. Bear the weaknesses of those without strength.
   b. Not to please ourselves.
2. By comforting them with the comfort that we receive from God.
3. a. Restore him in a spirit of gentleness.
   b. Bear one another's burdens.
4. His heart was broken, and He wept continually over their sin.
5. He wept over their sins.
6. He had great sorrow and unceasing grief.
7. With humility and tears and trials, but not shrinking back.

Correct Answers

Question No.	Answers

1. To suffer for His sake.
2. a. The world will hate us.
   b. They will persecute us.
   c. They shall separate you from their company (ostracize you).
   d. Shall cast insults at you.
   e. Spurn your name as evil.
3. We will be conformed to His death, and thus attain to the resurrection from the dead.
4. Keep on rejoicing.
5. The Spirit of glory and of God rests upon you.
6. Yes.
7. By the things which He suffered.
8. a. Through sufferings.
   b. No.
9. For us to follow.
10. a. Bear up under sorrows when suffering unjustly.
    b. Endure it patiently.
11. a. He did not revile in return.
    b. He uttered no threats.
    c. He entrusted Himself to Him who judges righteously.
    d. No.
12. a. If we suffer with Him, we will be glorified with Him.
    b. The sufferings now cannot be compared with the glory which shall be revealed to us.
13. The revealing of the sons of God.
14. a. You have not yet resisted to the point of shedding blood.
    b. God is dealing with us as the ones He loves.
    c. He scourges every son whom He receives.
    d. It is for discipline that you endure.
15. We are illegitimate children and not sons.
16. For our good, that we may share His holiness.
17. It will yield the peaceful fruit of righteousness.
18. To have perseverance and faith.
19. a. Now is come salvation.
    b. Now is come power.
    c. Now is come the kingdom of our God.
    d. Now is come the authority of His Christ.
20. a. By the blood of the Lamb.
    b. By the word of their testimony.
    c. And they did not love their life even to death.
21. We will sit with Jesus on His throne, even as He overcame and sat down with His Father on His throne.

SERIES I
BROKENNESS
STUDY 5—GOD'S PURPOSE IN TRIALS AND THE SPIRITUAL PROMISED LAND

Correct Answers

Question No.	Answers

1. To give them the land sworn to their fathers.
2. His ways are much higher.
3. a. Teaches you to profit.
   b. Leads you in the way you should go.
4. a. Consent and obey and eat the best of the land.
   b. Refuse and rebel and be devoured by the sword.
5. These things were written for our instruction.
6. We exult in hope of the glory of God.
7. Good land, of brooks of water, etc.
8. We shall reign in life as kings (Romans 6).
9. The old creation is buried and we are raised to walk in newness of life through what God does as a result of our faith at water baptism.
10. a. Made free from sin.
    b. Become enslaved to God.
    c. Fruit resulting in sanctification.
    d. The outcome is everlasting life.
11. a. To humble you.
    b. To test you.
    c. To know what is in your heart.
    d. To see if you will keep His commandments.
    e. To make you understand that man does not live by bread alone, but by the Word.
    f. God wants to discipline His sons.
    g. To see if you will walk in His ways and fear Him.
12. a. Great.
    b. Terrible.
    c. With fiery serpents.
    d. With scorpions.
    e. With thirsty ground (God's presence).
    f. With no water (Word goes dry).
    g. God brings water supernaturally.
13. a. Let us go up and possess it.
    b. For we shall surely overcome it.
    Evil Report:
    a. Can't go up against the people.
    b. They are stronger than us.
    c. There are giants in the land.
14. The people grumbled and wanted to return to Egypt.
15. a. The unbelievers did not see the land.
    b. God brought Caleb into the land.
16. He sees the promise, but is not really experiencing it.
17. He thanks God through Christ, as he is able to serve the law of God with his mind, but the law of sin with his flesh.
18. a. Fight the good fight of faith.
    b. Hold fast the confession of our hope without wavering.

19. 21 promises from Romans 8:
    1. (v. 1)   No condemnation.
    2. (v. 2)   Free from the law of sin and death.
    3. (v. 4)   Requirement of the law fulfilled in us—and we walk according to the Spirit.
    4. (v. 6)   We are spiritually minded.
    5. (v. 9)   The Spirit of God dwells in you.
    6. (v. 11)   Shall give life to our mortal bodies.
    7. (v. 13)   You will live—by putting to death the deeds of the body.
    8. (v. 14)   Led by the Spirit.
    9. (v. 15)   Received spirit of adoption.
    10. (v. 16)   The Spirit bears witness with our spirit that we are children of God.
    11. (v. 17)   Heirs of God—joint heirs with Christ.
    12. (v. 21)   Will receive glorious liberty.
    13. (v. 23)   Redemption of our bodies.
    14. (v. 26)   Spirit will help our weaknesses.
    15. (v. 28)   All things work together for good.
    16. (v. 29)   Predestined to be conformed to the image of His Son.
    17. (v. 31)   If God be for us—who can be against us?
    18. (v. 32)   He freely gives us all things.
    19. (v. 34)   Christ makes intercession for us.
    20. (v. 35)   Nothing shall separate us from the love of Christ.
    21. (v. 37)   We are more than conquerors.
20. Little by little.
21. a. So that you forget not the Lord thy God.
    b. So that thine heart not be lifted up.
22. With the great, with the strong.

Correct Answers

Question No.	Answers

1. We are a new creature; new things have come.
2. Old things are passed away.
3. We have passed from death unto life.
4. I am crucified with Christ, but Christ lives in me.
5. a. We must be united in the likeness of His death. This speaks of repentance, wherein we enter the Christian life through faith in Christ.
   b. 1. ' Putting Christ above your family.
      2. Taking up our cross daily.
      3. Forsaking all that we have.
   c. Death to sin, symbolized in water baptism.
6. a. Do not be bound together with unbelievers.
   b. Come out from among them (the worldly and ungodly).
   c. Be separate.
   d. Do not touch what is unclean (friendship with the world in enmity with God—James 4:4).
7. a. He will welcome us.
   b. He will be a Father to us.
   c. We shall be His sons and daughters.
8. No.
9. a. We shall also live with Him.
   b. We shall be in the likeness of His resurrection.
   c. We shall live with Him.
10. a. Consider them dead.
    b. Through faith in God who raised Christ and expressed at water baptism.
11. a. We are dead.
    b. Our life is hidden with Christ in God.
12. a. We are freed from sin.
    b. We have become slaves of righteousness.
13. No.
14. a. Once.
    b. No.
    c. Yes.
15. a. 1. Consider yourselves to be dead to sin.
       2. Consider yourselves to be alive to God.
    b. By faith.
16. Present yourselves to God, as those alive from the dead.
17. Abide in Christ and His Word.
18. No, No.
19. By Christ dwelling in our hearts *by faith*.
20. a. We enter into God's rest.
    b. Cease from our works.
21. Unbelief.
22. a. By letting His Word abide in us.
    b. By keeping His commandments.

23. The Spirit that raised up Jesus from the dead.
24. The life of Jesus.
25. He that is joined to the Lord is one spirit with Him.
26. a. Our minds are renewed.
    b. We have the mind of Christ.
27. a. 1. True.
       2. Honorable.
       3. Right.
       4. Pure.
       5. Lovely.
       6. Of good repute.
    b. God's Word.
28. Yes. (They are revealed unto us by His Spirit and are found in His Word. This is one reason we have received the Holy Spirit, that we might know the things He has given us.)
29. a. We must believe that He is.
    b. Believe He will reward us.
30. a. Speak the utterances of God.
    b. Avoid worldly and empty chatter.
    c. Offend not in word.
31. a. Joy.
    b. No, it will remain.
    c. By abiding in the vine.
32. a. That His joy may be fulfilled in us.
    b. No.
33. a. Condemnation. Experiencing jealousy and strife.
    b. Confess our sin.
34. To be conformed to the image of His Son.
35. a. Apostles.
    b. Prophets.
    c. Evangelists.
    d. Pastors.
    e. Teachers.
36. a. For the equipping of the saints.
    b. For the work of service.
37. a. Until we all attain to the unity of the faith.
    b. And to the knowledge of the Son of God.
    c. To a mature man.
    d. To the measure of the stature which belongs to the fulness of Christ.
38. That the church is without spot or wrinkle, being holy and blameless.

SERIES II
RIGHTEOUSNESS
STUDY 1—THE RIGHTEOUSNESS OF GOD

Correct Answers

Question No.	Answers

1. No.
2. Through the offering of the body of Jesus.
3. Once.
4. You must have faith.
5. The Lord Jesus, who shed His blood for us.
6. Through the blood sacrifice of Jesus.
7. Confess our sins. No.
8. a. Forgive our sins.
   b. Cleanse us from all unrighteousness.
9. All unrighteousness. Righteous and holy.
10. He was a man of unclean lips.
11. a. He confessed his sin.
    b. He mourned.
12. a. His iniquity was taken away.
    b. His sin was forgiven.
    c. It was taken away.
    d. Righteous.
13. No.
    a. Believed God took his sins away.
    b. Offered himself to God.
    c. No.
14. It is written, cursed is everyone who does not abide by all things written in the book of the law, to perform them.
15. No.
16. By faith in Christ's redemptive work.
17. He believed God.
18. No.
19. a. It was added because of transgressions.
    b. It was a tutor to bring us to Christ.
20. Until the seed should come—Jesus.
21. The New Covenant.
22. a. The law will be put in our minds and written upon our hearts.
    b. Fulfill the law.
23. a. A new creature.
    b. No.
24. a. Lay it aside.
    b. Through the spiritual experience signified and provided in water baptism.
    c. 1. Destroying speculations.
       2. Destroying every lofty thing raised up against the knowledge of God.
       3. Taking every thought captive to the obedience of Christ.
25. a. Put it on.
    b. 1. Be renewed in the spirit of your mind.
       2. Be renewed to a true knowledge according to the image of Him.
26. a. In righteousness.
    b. In holiness of the truth.
    Those similar to Jesus.

27. Walking in the Spirit.
28. a. We are dead to the law.
    b. We are joined to Christ.
    c. We shall bear fruit for God.
29. The law of sin and death.
30. Have faith.
31. a. Righteousness.
    b. Sin shall not be master over you.
    c. We are made free from sin.
    d. We have become servants to God.
    e. We have fruit, resulting in sanctification (see margin).
    f. We have everlasting life.
32. a. With confidence.
    b. With full assurance of faith.
    c. Having our hearts sprinkled from an evil conscience.
    d. Having our bodies washed with pure water.

SERIES II
RIGHTEOUSNESS
STUDY 2—THE RIGHTEOUSNESS THAT IS BY FAITH

Correct Answers

Question No.	Answers

1. a. Lawlessness.
   b. Darkness.
2. a. Fruit for death.
   b. Impurity.
   c. Lawlessness resulting in further lawlessness.
3. a. Experience like the tossing sea.
   b. Experience like the toss up of refuse and mud.
   c. No peace.
4. a. Has delivered us from the domain of darkness.
   b. Has transferred us to the kingdom of His beloved Son.
   c. We have redemption through His blood.
   d. Forgiveness of sins.
5. He was made sin for us.
   That we might be made the righteousness of God in Him.
6. He who has faith in Jesus.
7. To put away sin.
8. a. In righteousness.
   b. In holiness of the truth.
9. A new creature.
   It has passed away.
10. a. We are made free from sin.
    b. We become servants to God.
    c. We have fruit resulting in sanctification.
    d. The end—everlasting life.
11. Cleansed us from all sin and unrighteousness.
12. By faith.
13. By faith in Christ.
14. By faith.
15. Everything pertaining to life and godliness—through the true knowledge of Him.
16. Glory and virtue (or excellence).
17. By the precious and magnificent promises.
    The corruption that is in the world.
18. a. We are blind.
    b. We are shortsighted.
    c. Forgotten our purification from former sins.
19. a. You are fallen from grace.
    b. Nullify the grace of God.
20. Righteousness is reckoned to him who believes.
21. It is by faith, that it might be in accordance with grace.
22. There is no condemnation for those who are in Christ Jesus.
    Yes.
23. a. With a sincere heart.
    b. In full assurance of faith.
    c. Having our hearts sprinkled from an evil conscience.
    d. Having our bodies washed with pure water.

24. Yes.
    No.
25. God's.
26. Perfected for all time those who are sanctified.
27. a. Do not waver in unbelief.
    b. Be strong in faith.
    c. Give glory to God.
    d. Be fully assured that what He has promised He is able to perform.
    Righteousness.
    Hold fast the confession of our hope without wavering.

SERIES II
RIGHTEOUSNESS
STUDY 3—NEW CREATION REALITY

Correct Answers

Question No.	Answers

1. a. Deny ungodliness and worldly desires.
   b. Live sensibly, righteously and godly.
2. a. To redeem us from every lawless deed.
   b. To purify for Himself a people for His own possession.
   c. To have a people zealous for good deeds.
3. a. Made free from sin.
   b. Become enslaved to God.
   c. Fruit resulting in sanctification.
   d. Outcome—everlasting life.
   e. Qualified us to share in the inheritance.
   f. Delivered from darkness and transferred us into the kingdom of His beloved Son.
   g. Granted to us everything pertaining to life and godliness.
4. a. To righteousness.
   b. To holiness of the truth.
5. Because we are not renewed in the spirit of our mind.
6. Ignorance.
7. In our minds.
8. a. Be filled with the knowledge of His will in all spiritual wisdom and understanding.
   b. Walk worthy of the Lord.
   c. Bearing fruit in every good work.
   d. Increasing in the knowledge of God.
   e. Have a spirit of wisdom and revelation in the knowledge of Him.
   f. Eyes of your heart may be enlightened.
      1. To know what is the hope of His calling.
      2. To know the riches of the glory of His inheritance.
      3. To know what is the surpassing greatness of His power.
9. Be transformed by the renewing of your mind.
10. a. Renewed to a true knowledge.
    b. Made clean by the Word of the Lord Jesus.
11. Through the true knowledge of Him.
12. By His precious and magnificent promises.
13. a. Through faith.
    b. Through patience.
14. By faith.
15. They did not pursue it by faith.
16. Unbelief.
17. a. Put aside all filthiness and all that remains of wickedness.
    b. Receive with humility the Word implanted.
    c. Be doers of the Word, not hearers only.
18. a. Loins girded with truth.
    b. The mind.
19. Confess sin and be forgiven.
20. a. Look intently at the perfect law of liberty.
    b. Abide by it.
    c. Do not become a forgetful hearer.
    d. Be an effectual doer.

21. a. Blind; or short-sighted.
    b. Has forgotten his purification from his former sins.
22. By works.
23. Believed the promises of God—that God could even raise up Isaac from the dead.
24. Faith comes by hearing the Word of God.
25. a. The mind set on the flesh is death.
    b. The mind set on the Spirit is life and peace.
26. a. It is hostile toward God.
    b. It does not subject itself to the law of God.
    c. It cannot even be subjected to the law of God.
27. a. God sent His Son to condemn sin in the flesh.
    b. That the righteousness of the law might be fulfilled in those who walk according to the Spirit.
28. No.
29. We are being transformed into Christ's image.
30. His divine power through the true knowledge of Him has granted us these things.
31. a. Receive My words.
    b. Treasure My commandments within you.
    c. Make your ear attentive to wisdom.
    d. Incline your heart to understanding.
    e. Cry for discernment.
    f. Lift your voice for understanding.
    g. Search for her as silver and hidden treasures.
32. a. Righteousness.
    b. Justice.
    c. Equity and every good course.
33. From faith to faith.
34. a. Justice will dwell in the wilderness.
    b. Righteousness will abide in the fertile field.
35. a. Peace.
    b. Quietness.
    c. Confidence forever.
36. a. Shall hear what God will say.
    b. He shall speak peace to His people.
    c. He will not let them turn back to folly.
    d. His salvation shall be near.
    e. His glory may dwell in our land.
    f. Lovingkindness and truth have met together.
    g. Righteousness and peace have kissed each other.
    h. Truth springs from the earth.
    i. Righteousness looks down from heaven.
    j. God will give what is good.
    k. Righteousness will go before Him and make His footsteps into a way.

Correct Answers

Question No.	Answers

1. To be conformed to the image of His Son
2. From heaven.
3. God is love; we must love also.
4. He sent His only begotten Son into the world, that we might live through Him.
5. a. He first loved us.
   b. While we were yet sinners, Christ died for us.
   c. According to His mercy, He saved us.
6. a. Love one another.
   b. Abide in His love.
   c. Lay down your life for your friends.
7. Keep His commandments.
8. Love one another as Christ loves us.
9. His joy will be in us and our joy will be full.
10. a. Be born of God.
    b. By the Holy Ghost.
11. a. Seek our neighbor's good.
    b. Please your neighbor for his good, to his edification.
    c. Seek to profit many that they may be saved.
    d. Love your enemies.
    e. Do good to them that hate you.
    f. Bless them that curse you.
    g. Pray for those who mistreat you.
12. a. It is patient.
    b. It is kind.
    c. It is not jealous.
    d. It does not brag.
    e. It is not arrogant.
    f. It does not act unbecomingly.
    g. It does not seek its own.
    h. It is not provoked.
    i. It does not take into account a wrong suffered.
    j. It does not rejoice in unrighteousness.
    k. It rejoices in the truth.
    l. It bears all things.
    m. It believes all things.
    n. It hopes all things.
    o. It endures all things.
13. Yes.
14. The fulness of God.
15. Love never fails, that is, never ends.
16. We abide in God and God abides in us.
17. Our love is made perfect.

Correct Answers

Question No.	Answers

1. Life of praise and thanksgiving.
   a. By speaking to yourselves in psalms.
   b. By speaking to yourselves in hymns.
   c. By speaking to yourselves in spiritual songs.
   d. Singing and making melody with your heart.
   e. Giving thanks for all things.
2. In the infilling of the Spirit. Greek implies "go on being filled".
3. True worshipers, who worship Him in Spirit and in truth.
4. Because God is enthroned upon the praises of Israel.
5. Turned to God.
6. God's.
7. a. Station yourselves.
   b. Stand and see the salvation of the Lord on your behalf.
8. a. Put your trust in the Lord your God, and His prophets.
   b. Praise the Lord.
9. The Lord set ambushes against the enemies and they were destroyed.
10. Their grumbling.
11. Unbelief.
12. a. You shall serve your enemies.
    1. In hunger.
    2. In thirst.
    3. In nakedness.
    4. In the lack of all things.
    b. He will put an iron yoke on your neck.
    c. He shall destroy you.
13. a. A garland instead of ashes.
    b. The oil of gladness instead of mourning.
    c. The mantle of praise instead of a spirit of fainting.
    Praise glorifies the Lord.
14. Anointed with the oil of gladness above His companions.
15. That we might have His joy made full in us.
16. They had no song of praise.
17. a. We were like those who dream.
    b. Our mouth was filled with laughter.
    c. Our tongue was filled with joyful shouting.
18. They shall praise the Lord.
19. The whole assembly worshiped until the sacrifice was complete.
20. To sing praise in the midst of the congregation.
21. a. A sacrifice of praise to God.
    b. Continually.
22. They were as one—made one sound.
23. That we might be one.
24. a. Priests could not stand to minister because of the glory.
    b. The glory of the Lord filled the house.
25. a. Christ will be glorified in His saints.
    b. Christ will be marvelled at among all who have believed.

26. Praisers.
27. a. Sing to the Lord a new song.
    b. Praise Him in the congregation of the godly ones.
    c. Praise His name with dancing.
    d. Sing praises with the timbrel and lyre.
28. Sing for joy on your bed.
29. a. High praises of God in their mouth.
    b. A two-edged sword in their hand.
30. a. Execute vengeance on the nations.
    b. Punishment on the peoples.
    c. Bind their kings with chains.
    d. Bind their nobles with fetters of iron.
    e. Execute on them the judgment written.
    The nations will be brought into subjection to Christ, the enemy defeated, and the martyred saints will reign with Christ.
31. Speculations and every lofty thing raised up against the knowledge of God. And take every thought captive to the obedience of Christ.

Correct Answers

Question No.	Answers

1. By the Word of God, so that what is seen was not made out of what is visible.
2. The substance of things hoped for, the evidence of things not seen (see NAS margin).
3. It came to pass.
4. He calls into being that which does not exist.
5. If you believe that you will receive what you pray and ask for, they shall be granted you.
6. I speak just as the Father has told Me.
7. a. Be quick to hear.
   b. Slow to speak.
   c. Do not stumble in what we say.
   d. Speak the utterances of God.
8. Death and life are in the power of the tongue.
9. a. Hold fast the confession of our hope (faith) without wavering.
   b. Fight the good fight of faith.
10. a. See the promises.
    b. Welcome them from a distance.
    c. Confess you are a stranger on the earth (it is the promises of God that are real).
11. Tries to get us to doubt God's Word.
12. a. In hope against hope he believed.
    b. Without becoming weak in faith he considered the circumstances.
    c. He did not waver in unbelief.
    d. He grew strong in faith.
    e. He gave glory to God.
    f. He was fully assured that what God promised, He was able also to perform.
13. Righteousness.
14. No, it was written also for those who believe in Him.
15. a. To hold fast the confession of our hope without wavering.
    b. To have endurance.
16. Those who through faith and patience inherit the promises.
17. Rest.
18. For the faith that was once for all delivered to the saints.
19. a. The faith of Noah.
    b. The children of Israel passed through the Red Sea as though it were dry land.
    c. The walls of Jericho fell down by faith.
20. a. Lay aside every encumbrance and sin.
    b. Run with endurance the race that is set before us.
    c. Fix our eyes on Jesus the author and perfecter of faith.
21. Our faith.

Correct Answers

Question No.	Answers

1. If God is for us, who is against us?
2. Beloved, I pray that in all respects you may prosper and be in good health, just as your soul prospers.
3. Resist the devil and he will flee from you.
4. Give, and it will be given to you; good measure, pressed down, shaken together, running over.
5. They will lay hands on the sick and they will recover.
6. In My name they will cast out demons.
7. Because he has loved Me, therefore I will deliver him.
8. The Lord will fight for you while you keep silent.
9. It will come to pass that before they call, I will answer; and while they are still speaking, I will hear.
10. The prayer offered in faith will restore the one who is sick, and the Lord will raise him up, and if he has committed sins, they will be forgiven him.
11. Jesus Christ is the same yesterday and today, and forever.
12. Let it be done to you as you have believed.
13. Now thanks be to God, who always leads us in His triumph in Christ.
14. Call to Me, and I will answer you, and I will tell you great and mighty things, which you do not know.
15. These things I have spoken to you, that My joy may be in you, and that your joy may be made full.
16. Delight yourself in the Lord; and He will give you the desires of your heart.
17. But you shall receive power when the Holy Spirit has come upon you.
18. There is therefore now no condemnation for those who are in Christ Jesus.
19. No good thing does He withhold from those who walk uprightly.
20. If you abide in Me, and My words abide in you, ask whatever you wish, and it shall be done for you.
21. Blessed are the pure in heart, for they shall see God.
22. Casting all your anxiety upon Him because He cares for you.
23. He who offers a sacrifice of thanksgiving honors Me.
24. Until now you have asked for nothing in My name; ask, and you will receive, that your joy may be made full.
25. The steadfast of mind Thou wilt keep in perfect peace, because he trusts in Thee.
26. My God shall supply all your needs according to His riches in glory in Christ Jesus.
27. All things for which you pray and ask, believe that you have received them, and they shall be granted you.
28. For everyone who asks receives.
29. No evil will befall you, nor will any plague come near your tent.
30. Commit your way to the Lord, trust also in Him, and He will do it.

Correct Answers

Question No.	Answers

1. a. Full of futility.
   b. Understanding is darkened.
   c. Excluded from the life of God, because of the ignorance that is in them because of a hardened heart.
2. a. How long will you love simplicity?
   b. How long will you delight in scoffing and hate knowledge?
3. a. If we turn, He will pour out His Spirit on us.
   b. He will make His Words known to us.
4. a. They hated knowledge (spiritual knowledge).
   b. Did not choose the fear of the Lord.
   c. Would not accept His counsel.
   d. They spurned all the Lord's reproof.
5. a. We shall live securely.
   b. We shall be at ease from the dread of evil.
6. a. Acquire wisdom.
   b. Get understanding.
7. a. She will exalt you.
   b. She will honor you.
   c. She shall place on your head a garland of grace.
   d. She will present you with a crown of beauty.
   e. The years of your life will be many.
8. Watch over your heart with all diligence, for from it flow the springs of life.
9. a. He will guide us into all truth.
   b. He will not speak on His own initiative, but what He hears from the Father, disclosing to us what is Jesus'.
   c. He will disclose to us what is to come.
   a. He will answer us.
   b. He will tell us great and mighty things which we do not know.
10. Seek the Lord while He may be found; call upon Him while He is near.
11. a. A man lacking sense.
    b. Over grown with thistles and nettles (the cares of this life).
    c. Stone wall was broken down.
12. Laziness.
13 a. Let us not sleep.
    b. Let us be alert and sober.
    c. Put on the breastplate of faith and love.
    d. Put on the helmet of salvation.
14. He who has and keeps My commandments is loved by My Father, and I love him and will disclose Myself to him.
15. He will come in as the King of glory.
16. a. Meditate on it day and night.
    b. Be careful to do all that is written in it.
    a. Your way will be prosperous.
    b. You will have success.
17. Let the Word of Christ richly dwell within you.
18. Ask whatever you wish and it shall be done for you.

19. a. Trust in the Lord with all your heart.
    b. Do not lean on your own understanding.
    c. In all your ways acknowledge Him.
    d. He will make your paths straight.
20. a. Pure.
    b. Peaceable.
    c. Gentle.
    d. Reasonable.
    e. Full of mercy.
    f. Full of good fruits.
    g. Unwavering.
    h. Without hypocrisy.
21. a. He will grant us to be strengthened with power through His Spirit in the inner man.
    b. That Christ may dwell in our hearts through faith.
    c. To be rooted and grounded in love.
    d. That we may comprehend with all the saints what is the breadth and length and height and depth.
    e. To know the love of Christ.
    f. To be filled with all the fulness of God.
22. Glory.

Correct Answers

Question No.	Answers

1. To proclaim the kingdom of God and to perform healing.
2. The kingdom of God.
3. a. He laid His hands on them and healed them.
   b. Demons came out of many.
4. a. Go into all the world and preach the gospel to all creation.
   b. Proclaim repentance for forgiveness of sins in His name to all nations.
   c. Go and make disciples of all nations, baptizing them.
   d. Teach them (all nations) to observe all that I have commanded you.
5. Stay in the city until you are clothed with power from on high.
6. They were to receive power.
7. a. To preach the gospel to the poor.
   b. To proclaim release to the captives.
   c. To proclaim recovery of sight to the blind.
   d. To set free those who are downtrodden.
   e. To proclaim the favorable year of the Lord.
8. Yes.
9. a. To serve.
   b. To give His life a ransom for many.
10. a. Be a servant.
    b. Be a slave.
    c. Keep the commandments of the Lord.
    d. Teach the commandments.
11. In giving.
12. As each one has received a gift, employ it in serving one another.
13. God has made us adequate as servants of a new covenant.
    The Spirit.
14. A ministry of glory.
15. a. With great boldness in our speech.
    b. Minister with an open face (unveiled).
16. We do not lose heart.
17. a. The Lord.
    b. The Spirit of Him that raised Jesus from the dead.
18. a. No—Christ Jesus the Lord.
    b. No—The power of God.
19. a. Your light will rise in darkness.
    b. Your gloom will become like midday.
    c. The Lord will continually guide you.
    d. He will satisfy your desire in scorched places.
    e. He will give strength to your bones.
    f. You will be like a watered garden.
    g. You will be like a spring of water whose waters do not fail.
20. No—We are complete in Him.
21. a. His fulness (Note: This refers to the fulness of revelation of the Incarnate Word).
    b. Grace upon grace.
    c. The mind of Christ.

22. a. Love.
    b. Joy.
    c. Peace.
    d. Patience.
    e. Kindness.
    f. Goodness.
    g. Faithfulness.
    h. Gentleness.
    i. Self-control.
23. a. Love.
    b. Joy.
    c. Peace.
    d. Patience.
    e. Kindness.
    f. Goodness.
    g. Faithfulness.
    h. Gentleness (humility).
    i. Self-control.

Correct Answers

Question No.	Answers

1. a. Word of wisdom.
   b. Word of knowledge.
   c. Faith.
   d. Gifts of healing.
   e. Effecting of miracles.
   f. Prophecy.
   g. Distinguishing of spirits.
   h. Various kinds of tongues.
   i. Interpretation of tongues.
2. a. Prophecy.
   b. Tongues.
   c. Interpretation of tongues.
   a. Word of wisdom.
   b. Word of knowledge.
   c. Distinguishing of spirits.
   a. Faith.
   b. Gifts of healing.
   c. Effecting of miracles.
3. For the common good.
4. No.
5. a. Pursue love.
   b. Desire spiritual gifts, especially prophecy.
6. Kindle afresh the gift of God which is in you.
7. To edify the church.
8. Rather that we prophesy unless we have interpretation with tongues.
9. a. Edifies.
   b. Exhorts.
   c. Consoles.
10. a. He is convicted by all.
    b. He is called to account by all.
    c. The secrets of his heart are disclosed.
    d. He will fall on his face and worship God.
    e. Declare that God is certainly among you.
11. The spirit of prophecy.
12. He who believes in Me, from his innermost being shall flow rivers of living water.
13. The power that created the world.
14. Raised a child from the dead.
    Divided the waters.
15. Fed one hundred men with twenty loaves of barley and some fresh ears of grain.
    He cleansed the leper.
16. A dead man touched his bones and was revived.

Correct Answers

Question No.	Answers

1. a. You are a slave to the one you obey.
   b. You become enslaved.
2. a. The love of the world.
   b. Love of the things in the world.
      1. Lust of the flesh.
      2. Lust of the eyes.
      3. The boastful pride of life.
3. Devination (witchcraft).
   Iniquity and idolatry.
4. God visits the iniquity of the fathers on the children, and on the third and fourth generation of those who hate Him.
5. a. God will destroy him.
   b. In the way you judge, you will be judged.
   c. By your standard of measure, it will be measured to you.
6. a. Commit your way unto the Lord.
   b. Trust in Him.
   c. He will do it.
7. a. Sluggard (lazy).
   One lacking sense.
   b. Overwork.
      1. He will make us ride on the heights of the earth.
      2. He will feed us with the heritage of Jacob.
8. a. By your words you shall be justified.
   b. By your words you shall be condemned.
   a. A snare—by the transgression of our lips.
   b. The righteous will escape from trouble.
   c. By the fruit of our words we will be satisfied with good.
   d. The tongue of the wise brings healing.
   e. The one who guards his mouth preserves his life.
   f. The one who opens wide his lips comes to ruin.
   g. A soothing tongue is a tree of life.
   h. Perversion on the tongue crushes the spirit.
9. If you hate your brother.
10. Do not sin anymore.
11. The spirit comes back in and brings seven other spirits more evil than itself, and the last state becomes worse than the first.
12. Love.
13. You must forgive.
14. God will hand us over to the torturers if we forgive not.
15. Confess your sins to one another and pray for one another.
    a. He is faithful and righteous to forgive us our sins.
    b. And to cleanse us from all unrighteousness.
16. a. The blood of the Lamb.
    b. The word of our testimony.
    c. We love not our lives even to death.
17. Walk in the light as He is in the light.

18. Keep His Word.
19. a. It is earthly, natural (unspiritual).
    b. It is demonic.
    c. There is disorder.
    d. There is every evil thing.
    a. Pure.
    b. Peaceable.
    c. Gentle.
    d. Reasonable.
    e. Full of mercy.
    f. Full of good fruits.
    g. Unwavering.
    h. Without hypocrisy.
20. a. Speak to one another in psalms and hymns and spiritual songs.
    b. Singing and making melody in your heart.
    c. Always giving thanks for all things.
21. The believer through Christ.
22. No.
23. In the synagogue.
24. What is this? A new teaching with authority!
25. a. It recognized Jesus and spoke to Him.
    b. It threw the man it was in into convulsions.
    c. It cried out with a loud voice.
26. He casts out demons by the ruler of demons.
27. A house divided against itself cannot stand. So, if Satan casts out Satan, how shall his kingdom stand?
28. The kingdom of God has come upon you.
29. Yes.
30. Eyes are full of darkness.
31. Whatever you shall bind on earth shall be bound in heaven, and whatever you shall loose on earth shall be loosed in heaven.

Correct Answers

Question No.	Answers

1. a. Make disciples of all nations.
    b. Baptize them.
    c. Teach them to observe all that He has commanded us.
2. His glory, glory as of the only begotten from the Father.
3. Speak the words of God without fear.
4. Being a bond-servant of Christ.
5. a. Cry loudly.
    b. Do not hold back.
    c. Raise your voice like a trumpet.
    d. Declare to My people their transgression.
6. Stand in God's council.
7. a. Walk with integrity.
    b. Work righteousness.
    c. Speak truth in the heart.
    d. Do not slander.
    e. Do not do evil to a neighbor or friend.
    f. Despise a reprobate, and honor those who fear the Lord.
    g. Swear to your own hurt (no matter the cost, you will fulfill your word).
    h. Do not lend at interest or take bribes.
8. a. Teach people the difference between the holy and the profane.
    b. Cause them to discern between the unclean and the clean.
9. Do not omit a word.
10. a. Do not say, 'I am a youth.'
    b. Do not be afraid of them.
    c. Do not be dismayed before them, lest I dismay you before them.
11. a. Neither fear them nor fear their words.
    b. Speak My words whether they listen or not.
    c. Do not be rebellious.
12. a. I have made you as a fortified city.
    b. I have made you as an iron pillar.
    c. I have made you as walls of bronze.
    d. They will fight against you, but they will not overcome you.
    e. I have made your face as hard as their faces.
    f. I have made your forehead as hard as their foreheads.
13. a. Relate his dream.
    b. Speak God's Word in truth.
14. a. Like fire.
    b. Like a hammer which shatters a rock.
15. a. Those who steal His words from each other.
    b. Those who use their tongues and declare, "The Lord declares."
    c. Those who have prophesied false dreams.

16. a. Be diligent to present yourself approved to God, handling accurately the word of truth.
    b. Avoid worldly and empty chatter.
    c. Flee from youthful lusts.
    d. Pursue righteousness, faith, love, and peace.
    e. Refuse foolish and ignorant speculations.
    f. Be kind to all, able to teach and patient when wronged.
    g. With gentleness correcting those who are in opposition.
17. a. Suffer hardship.
    b. Do not entangle yourself in the affairs of everyday life.
    c. Compete according to the rules.

Correct Answers

Question No.	Answers

1. They immediately left everything and followed Him.
2. They paid no attention to it and went their own ways (interested more in the cares of this life).
3. Many are called, but few are chosen.
4. a. These who have not been defiled with women, they kept themselves chaste.
   b. They follow the Lamb wherever He goes.
   c. No lie was found in their mouth.
   d. They are blameless.
   e. They are the called and chosen and faithful.
5. a. Be a servant.
   b. Be a slave.
6. a. He did not count his life dear to himself.
   b. That he might finish his course.
   c. He declared the whole purpose of God.
7. a. Fools for Christ's sake, weak and without honor.
   b. Hungry and thirsty, poorly clothed, roughly treated, and are homeless.
   c. Toiled, working with their own hands.
   d. When reviled, they bless.
   e. When persecuted, they endure.
   f. When slandered, they try to conciliate.
   g. They became as the scum of the world, the dregs of all things.
8. They gave no offense in anything, but in all the things listed they commended themselves as servants of God.
9. a. Not from error or impurity or by way of deceit.
   b. Not as pleasing men but God.
   c. Not with flattering speech, nor with a profit for good.
   d. Not seeking glory from men.
   e. Gentle, as a nursing mother tenderly cares for her own children.
   f. Imparted their own lives.
   g. Labored night and day.
   h. Behaved themselves devoutly, uprightly, and blamelessly.
   i. Exhorted, encouraged and implored as a father would his own son.
10. a. Ambassadors for Christ.
    b. Angels of the Church.
    c. Fishers of men.
    d. Defenders of the gospel.
    e. Fellow workers in the gospel.
    f. Lamps.
    g. Men of God.
    h. Messengers of the Lord of hosts.
    i. Priests of the Lord and ministers of God.
    j. Ministers of the sanctuary.
    k. Servants of righteousness.
    l. Soldiers of Christ.
    m. Stars.
    n. Stewards of the grace of God.
    o. Stewards of the mysteries of God.

Correct Answers

Question No.	Answers

1. a. Priests of the Lord.
   b. Ministers of our God.
2. a. To comfort all who mourn.
   b. To give them a garland instead of ashes.
   c. To give them the oil of gladness.
   d. To give them the mantle of praise.
3. a. They will rebuild the ancient ruins.
   b. Raise up the former devastations.
   c. Repair the ruined cities.
   d. The desolations of many generations.
4. a. Be devoted to one another in brotherly love.
   b. Give preference to one another in honor.
5. a. All day and all night never keep silent.
   b. You take no rest.
   c. Give Him no rest until He establishes "Jerusalem" a praise in the earth.
6. a. Go through the gates.
   b. Clear the way for the people.
   c. Build up the highway.
   d. Remove the stones.
   e. Lift up a standard over the peoples.
7. Warn and help the people.
8. The people, if they have been warned.
9. The watchman.
10. Never.
11. a. Lay down our lives for the brethren.
    b. Give of your goods to those in need.
    c. Love in deed and truth.
12. Be a servant of all.
13. a. They will have a double portion.
    b. Everlasting joy will be theirs.
    c. The Lord will faithfully give them their recompense.
    d. The Lord will make an everlasting covenant with them.
14. The offspring whom the Lord has blessed.

Life Changing Books
& Bible Studies
from Maranatha Publications

Bible Study Series

Firm Foundation

This study is our best seller. Covers the foundational truths in Scripture. Includes repentance, baptism, healing, faith, and other studies. Paperback, 125 pages, $11.95
ISBN # 0-938553-005

Overcoming Life

Takes you a step further than the basics. Includes a series on brokenness, as well as faith, righteousness, and the work of the ministry. Paperback, 113 pages, $11.95
ISBN # 0-938558-01-3

Lovers of God

Life Changing truths from Philippians. The all-sufficiency of God, living in joy, victory over trials, having the mind of Christ, and fruitfulness in ministry. Paperback, 43 pages, $9.95
ISBN # 0-938558-03-X

Preparation of the Bride

Explains metaphors and hidden truths in the Song of Solomon. This study reveals the beauty of the union between Jesus and His Bride. Paperback, 234 pages, $16.95
ISBN # 0-88270-471-0

Life of Excellence

Help for building character in your Christian life… bridling the tongue, godly wisdom, our attitude toward sinners, living in the last days, and more. Paperback, 60 pages, $9.95
ISBN # 0-938558-04-8

Estudios Biblicos para un Fundamento Firmé

Firm Foundation Also Available in Spanish!

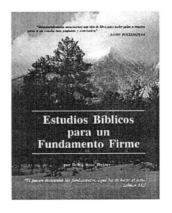

An interactive Bible Study that challenges the reader to utilize their Bible and seek out truths in Scripture. This top selling Bible study is used around the world. Paperback, 125 pages, $11.95
ISBN # 0-938558-22-6

Life Changing Historical Reprints

from Maranatha Publications

The Story of Liberty

originally published in 1879.

The secular humanists have edited God out of history! Now you can read what they cut out. Reprinted from the original 1879 edition, *The Story of Liberty* tells you the price that was paid for our freedom and how it was won. An excellent historical resource for your library. This is our best seller among home schools and Christian educators. Paperback, illustrated, 415 pages, $14.95 ISBN 0-938558-20-X

The Story of Liberty Study Guide – Written by Steve Dawson,

this workbook offers 98 pages of challenging comprehensive questions that allow the reader to fill-in-the-blank as they progress through this valuable study book. $10.95 ISBN 0-938558-27-7

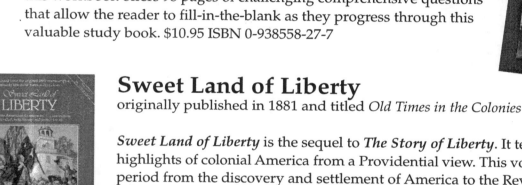

Sweet Land of Liberty

originally published in 1881 and titled *Old Times in the Colonies*

Sweet Land of Liberty is the sequel to *The Story of Liberty*. It tells the historical highlights of colonial America from a Providential view. This volume covers the period from the discovery and settlement of America to the Revolutionary War. Written by Civil War correspondent and children's author Charles Coffin, *Sweet Land of Liberty* has been faithfully reproduced exactly as it was originally printed in 1881. Paperback, illustrated, 458 pages, $14.95 ISBN 0-938558-48-X

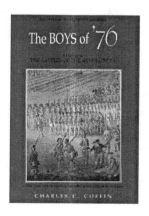

The Boys of '76

reprinted from the original 1876 manuscript

In this powerful volume an attempt has been made to give a concise, plain, and authentic narrative of the principal battles of the Revolution as witnessed by those who took part in them. More than a century has passed since "*The Boys of '76*" shouldered their muskets and fought for their liberties. Author Charles Coffin brings to life the battles of the Revolution from "The Alarm" proclaimed in Concord in 1775, to the surrender of the British army in 1981. Paperback, illustrated, 423 pages, $16.95. ISBN 0-938558-82-X

"An accurate story of our nation's fight for liberty. I pray everyone, young and old alike, will read and remember *The Boys of '76*."

Greg Harris, Director of Noble Institute and author of *The Christian Home School*

Christian Perspectives

Biblical Views on Important Issues

These books are inspiring resources for Christian educators and all who want to challenge themselves to think and act on subjects of intellectual and social concern.

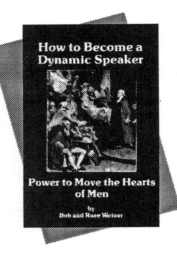

How to Become a Dynamic Speaker
by Bob & Rose Weiner

Christians are called to be the greatest communicators in the world. Do you desire to speak fearlessly with power to move the hearts of men? This book offers inspiring, practical advice that will help you become a more effective communicator.

paperback, 19 pages, $2.50
ISBN 0-938558-19-6

Mightier Than the Sword
by Bob & Rose Weiner

This book emphasizes the value of writing to develop the thinking and reasoning processes as well as offers practical suggestions to help you learn how to give written expression to your inner thoughts.

paperback, 20 pages, $2.50
ISBN 0-938558-16-1

Christian Dominion: The Legacy of Early America
by Bob & Rose Weiner

This book presents the mandate for Christian dominion which enabled our founders to build a nation unlike any other in the history of the world.

paperback, 27 pages, $2.50
ISBN 0-938558-10-2

More Christian Perspectives
Biblical Views on Important Issues
These books are thought provoking treatments of various issues including
Christian economics and literature.

The Bed is Too Short
by Bob & Rose Weiner
The children's story of the tortoise and the hare has much
spiritual application. Practical advice on how to develop a
sensitivity to the still small voice of God and how to rise
above your circumstances and walk in God's grace.
paperback, 35 pages, $2.50
ISBN 0-938558-08-8

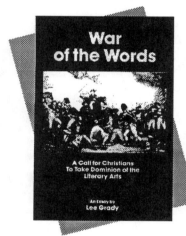

War of the Words
by Lee Grady
Humanists and atheists have affected society through
literature while Christians have had little influence in this field.
This book offers a challenge for Christians to take dominion of
the literary arts.
paperback, 18 pages, $2.50
ISBN 0-938558-11-0

Defending Christian Economics
by Lee Grady
This book examines the Biblical system of economics - individual
enterprise - and looks at the Christian solution to poverty. This
message is an important weapon in the battle against Marxist
philosophy.
paperback, 26 pages, $2.50
ISBN 0-938558-12-9

A Vision for World Dominion
by Lee Grady
The two articles in this book, "Where Will We Be in the Year
2025?" and "The Forgotten Progress of the Gospel" remind us
that Jesus Christ intends to rule planet earth and to pour out
His Spirit in world-wide revival.
paperback, 21 pages, $2.50
ISBN 0-938558-13-7

MARANATHA PUBLICATIONS, INC.

P. O. BOX 1799 • GAINESVILLE, FL 32602 • 352-375-6000 • FAX 352-335-0080

Bible Study Books— *by Bob and Rose Weiner*

BOOK NAME	PRICE	QUANTITY	TOTAL
Firm Foundation	$ 11.95		
Overcoming Life	$ 11.95		
Lovers of God	$ 9.95		
Life of Excellence	$ 9.95		
Preparation of the Bride	$16.95		
One Set of Above Studies (5)	$55.75		
Jesus Brings New Life	$ 5.95		
Spanish Firm Foundation	$ 11.95		

Christian History Books

BOOK NAME	PRICE	QUANTITY	TOTAL
The Story of Liberty (A Christian History Text)	$14.95		
Story of Liberty Study Guide - by Steve Dawson	$ 10.95		
Sweet Land of Liberty (Sequel to Story of Liberty)	$14.95		
The Boys of '76 (Sequel to Sweet Land of Liberty)	$16.95		

Booklets

BOOK NAME	PRICE	QUANTITY	TOTAL
— by Bob and Rose Weiner			
How to Become a Dynamic Speaker	$ 2.50		
Mightier Than The Sword	$ 2.50		
The Bed Is Too Short	$ 2.50		
Christian Dominion	$ 2.50		
— by Lee Grady			
Defending Christian Economics	$ 2.50		
A Vision For World Dominion	$ 2.50		
War of the Words	$ 2.50		

Sub Total	
Shipping	
Add FL sales tax	
TOTAL US Dollars	

VISA and MasterCard Accepted

Ship To:

Name _____

Address _____

City _____

State _____ Zip _____

Phone (_____) _____

❏ Check enclosed, payable to Maranatha Publications, Inc.

❏ Charge to my: ❏ VISA ❏ MasterCard

Card No. _____ Expires ___/___

Shipping & Handling:

Less than $10.00	$3.50
$10.00 - $24.99	$4.50
$25.00 - $49.99	$5.50
$50.00 or more	9%

Mail Order To: **Maranatha Publications, Inc., P.O. Box 1799, Gainesville, FL 32602**
Visit our websie at www.mpi2000.net